30 Ways to Love Maryland

2019 Anthology
Maryland Writers' Association

Edited by Katherine Melvin

A Maryland Writers' Association Book

Copyright 2019 by the Maryland Writers' Association

All rights reserved. No part of this book may be used or reproduced in any manner without written permission from the Maryland Writers' Association.

Published in the United States of America by
MWA Books, a division of the Maryland Writers' Association
3 Church Circle, # 165
Annapolis, MD 21401
www.marylandwriters.org

ISBN 978-0-9820032-6-8
Cover design by Katherine Melvin
Interior design by Eileen McIntire

First Edition

Contents

FOREWORD by Katherine Melvin, Editor - 5

SHORT STORIES -7
The Decision by Anita Meredith -9
A Love Letter to Maryland by Meredith Johnson - 15
Autumn Island by Emmy Nicklin - 21
By the River by FJ Talley - 31
Tropical Storm by Kevin Lavey - 39
The Bar on Infinity Street by Leona Upton Illig - 48
Welcome Homesick by Rissa Miller - 59
Love Among the Black-eyed Susans by Beth Smith - 71
Patti and The SUN by Melisa Peterson Lewis - 82
Tilly and the Sykesville Sasquatch by Melisa Peterson Lewis - 90
Seven Postcards From My Unmarried Aunt Betsy Plus One Letter by Ellen Krawczak - 100
Baltimore: Life on the Streets by Suzanne McCoskey - 104

ESSAYS - 107
Sailing The Chesapeake by Daniel Rosenblum - 109
A Foot In Both Worlds by T.J. Butler - 114
The Bridge by Donna Rothert - 125
Crabtown by Linda Wood - 130
Once Upon A Dream In Maryland by Linda Wood - 134
Muskrat Love by Bronwyn Mitchell-Strong - 139
Fireballs, Tsunamis, Volcanoes—Oh My! by Edna Troiano - 150

Welcome To Maryland by Jane Newhagen - 154
Celebrating Crab Mechanics by Donna Rothert - 157
Autumn, Crossing The Chesapeake by Donna Rothert - 162
You're Probably A Southern Marylander If . . . by Liz Cooper - 167

MEMOIRS - 177
Chasing A Murderer by James Burd Brewster - 179
Shallow Roots by Theresa Wood - 184
Lawbreakers by Aly Parsons -195
"We Don't Have A Head Of Household:" Collective Living In Baltimore by Fred Pincus - 198
Maryland, My Maryland by Margaret Warfield - 219
The Tribes Of Port Baltimore by Walter Curran - 215
Christmas Eve Celebration by Joanne Zaslow - 224
Greek Easter Bash by Joanne Zaslow - 227
Baltimore Fairytale by Karen R.Roberts - 229

Foreword

When I undertook the task of running the Maryland Writers' Association 30th Anniversary Anthology Contest, I didn't realize just how interesting an experience it would be. Being a glass half-empty person, I wondered if we'd receive thirty entries let alone thirty publishable ones. To my delight, I learned Maryland is filled with incredibly talented writers! There were so many great essays, memoirs, and short stories all cleverly told that it was difficult to cull out the thirty best ones. So much so, we found it necessary to include thirty-two.

While I've lived here almost thirty years and call the state home, I learned a lot from the submissions. Marylanders are very, very picky about their crab picking and eating procedures. Don't mess with them. We love the Bay and The Bridge, no need to clarify which bridge to a Marylander. The beautiful landscape spreads east from the stunning seashore to the expansive mountains surrounding Deep Creek Lake, urban chic to tranquil country, and American history at its best, and its worst.

Come with me on this adventure called 30 Ways to Love Maryland. Experience the state, enjoy the humor, the history, and the ingenuity shown in each piece. It's a wonderful journey, just right for reading on a lazy day at the beach or holed up inside in front a fire on a cold winter's day.

Thank you to the judges: Kathryn Johnson, Bertie S. Bryant, and Dr. Janeula Burt. These talented women were gracious enough to slug through sixty-four entries with no complaints! You are the best!

Thank you to the Maryland Writers' Association Board who supported, cheered, and sometimes prodded the project along. It's been an honor to serve with you.

>Katherine Melvin, Editor
>MWA Program Chair

Katherine Melvin is a D.C.-based writer. Her short stories and articles have appeared in *Beach Days*, the *2014 MWA Anthology, Today's Christian Women, Christianity Today*, and *Catholic Digest.* She is currently at work on a humorous series titled *The Tales of Mud Creek*. She is a past president of the MWA Montgomery Chapter and serves as Program Chair at the state level.

Short Stories

The Decision
By Anita Meredith

She looks through the window of her living room at the endless green grass and the shimmering water of the Chesapeake Bay just beyond her door. She glances back inside at her phone that she has placed on the table beside her. She considers for a moment what her life would be like if she moved away from this place. It is difficult to imagine. How can she move away when most of her life has centered so solidly on her surroundings in this, her Maryland home? Can she possibly consider such a thing?

Ever since she was a small child she has been a part of this state and it is where she has spent her formative years. She can hardly remember a time when she was not a part of this place. Her roots are here, and, like breathing, it feels easy and natural. She scarcely remembers the harsher landscape of her Southern most home before her parents moved her at a young age to Baltimore, back to the place where they grew up.

She thinks of the things that she would miss the most, but it is impossible to narrow down. There are thirty reasons and more why she loves Maryland. Remembering the anticipation of early spring and the arrival of the migrating orioles, both the colorful state bird and the Oriole baseball team returning from a winter spent in warmer climates, she smiles to herself. And how can she forget the winter team named after a different bird, a bird that is deeply rooted in the history of a Baltimore literary legend? A Baltimore legend that has endured and retained its mystery throughout the decades with the celebration of three red roses left on his gravestone each anniversary of his birth.

She steps outside her back door and walks for a while. As she approaches the shoreline, she thinks how she would mourn the loss of the peace that comes from living so near to the water. And the respect that she knows the water deserves when the weather suddenly turns deadly. For many years she has taken for granted the good things that come from living so close to the shore, the ability to drive less than a few hours to walk along the sand beside the mighty ocean or simply to be near the rivers and the Chesapeake Bay with its abundant sea life, blue crabs and shore birds. She appreciates the beauty of the many lighthouses shining their beacons of light to safely guide travelers through treacherous waters. She adores the sounds that the water makes and the rhythmic gentle rushing of the sand and the waves beneath her toes. This nearness to the great bodies of waters is probably one of the things she loves most about her home state. But she also relishes the thought that a short trip in the opposite direction will take her to beautiful mountain retreats, hiking trails and spectacular waterfall falls.

Can she really just leave the only home that she has come to know and love behind? She walks slowly and silently along the familiar path outside her house and wonders if she should change her path to something a little less familiar, less comfortable.

-2-

The job offer that she has received from a very promisingtech forward company out west is an enticing one, one that she is considering carefully. This kind of opportunity comes only once in a lifetime. Her friends and colleagues keep reminding her of this.

She continues on her way, following the path back around to her door and returns inside. Her phone sits waiting on the table where she left it. She contemplates pressing the dial button, but she hesitates. Something stops her. She holds the phone for a long time as she gazes at the screen, distracted by the pictures that she has recently taken on it.

For a few moments she stares at the pictures there. Like the inside of a black hole, they draw her in. These are the photos that she took of the place that would be her new home out west, with its beautiful red landscape and carved rock formations, but all she feels is, well, thirsty. Where is the green? The varied and subtle shades of leaves and the wind swept grassy fields? She swipes through the pictures on her phone over and over. Every picture from her visit while she traveled for the interview, although beautiful in its own way, is also dry and dusty, and thirsty-looking.

She pushes aside the photos from her trip out west and sighs as she pulls out a different set of photos and with them a different set of memories. These photos, lovingly collected over the years, are filled with the history of this place which is her home in Maryland. The history displayed on the pages of this album reaches out to her across the decades, connecting her not just with Maryland's past but also with her family's roots.

Her smile widens as she remembers her family's stories. Hers is a family that loves to tell its stories gathered around kitchen tables and campfires. She would miss her family most of all. How she loves to listen to the telling of their stories. Tales of her ancestors who watched while the sky was ablaze with gun powder and witnessed the same sky as Francis Scott Key, the night he wrote a song for our country. Stories of how her ancestors came to America so long ago with nothing but a few articles of clothing and a dream of a better life.

   She sits quietly at the table and opens the photo album, spreading its contents across the tabletop in front of her. She flips through the pages, brimming with family photos of Assateague Island camping trips and visits to the Ocean City Boardwalk. Happy, sun-burned faces fill the pages. To this day she has not lost her childlike joy, waiting for summer's arrival and the trips to watch the ponies of Assateague, running wild alongside the shores of the Atlantic. These wild ponies, the inspiration for her favorite Maryland literary tale, have given her yet another reason to love her home state. This story is rich with the description and the passion of this unique place. A story loved by generations of children. Thinking of this connection to her childhood, her family and her home in Maryland, tugs unexpectedly at her heart.

-3-

   She turns the page again and finds yet another collection of photos filled with the memories of her family's visit to a Pre-Revolutionary farm house. As she looks at them she feels the weight of a past come to life in this old home where it is believed meetings were held to plot and plan the revolution of an emerging American people. She feels the essence of their passionate determination to declare their independence and to become a new nation. The images on the pages are filled with a powerful and almost palpable sense of purpose. A life lived in another era reaches out to the present day. Even still, the memory of this farm and the people who lived there haunts her dreams. Their hopes, their struggles, reach out to her and beg for their stories to be known.

   All of these places and events, so dear to her, nearly

dance off the pages in front of her. Their images demand her attention as she leafs further into the album. Pictures of friends at crab feasts, enjoying anything and everything food-related that is sprinkled with Old Bay seasoning, or J.O. Spice. These spices, like the spicy Hons of Baltimore and the dazzling Christmas lights of the Miracle on 34th Street in Hampden, have become faithful friends, always an integral part of the area and its traditions. There are photos of grand events such as the much-loved and highly anticipated Preakness Stakes, but there are also reminders of much simpler days like the ones spent at a Maryland farm where thoroughbred horses are raised and trained. Photos of field trips to Annapolis and the Naval Academy spring from the pages of her album. The smiling faces of her classmates call to her as they stand posing on the steps of the State Capitol Building with its rich history, once serving as the Capitol of our nation. The pages display memories of sailing ships proudly flying the distinctive state flag, fishing boats on the Chesapeake Bay, and farm produce from the Eastern Shore which fill the stalls at the local farmers' market to overflowing.

    She turns away from the pages before her. It is too much to take in. Memories made and treasures of a lifetime stand there.

    She glances back at her phone and takes a deep breath, preparing herself to dial the number that could change her life. As she reaches for the phone, it begins to ring as if on cue. Startled, she draws her hand away from the phone. A familiar number blinks on the screen, impatient for her answer. For a moment she considers letting her voicemail pick up, but then thinks better of it. After all, she has made her decision. Drawing in an even deeper breath, she gathers herself and picks up the phone call.

ANITA MEREDITH is the author of the children's chapter book, *Dudley and the Mud Monster.* Her work is included in the Carroll County Chapter of the MWA's anthology, *In Short: A Selection of Short Fiction from Carroll County Writers.* A graduate of Towson University, she lives with her family and her Angora rabbits on a small farm in Maryland. An avid reader, she also enjoys fiber arts and gardening. *(Photo credit: MellPiccoDesign)*

A Love Letter to Maryland
By Meredith Johnson

The rain was falling hard, increasing the chill Emma felt from the fall weather that had finally settled in. It was October, her favorite time of year. The summer seemed to be prolonged by the never-ending heat of September and she was glad to be back in sweatpants enjoying a cup of hot tea. The storm would last off and on all weekend according to the weather man, and that was just fine by Emma who hadn't made plans anyway. The summer had kept her busy. Between trips with her best friends and the trips she and her husband made, there hadn't been a moment to sit and relax. Not that she was complaining. All of it had been fun and memorable. Her husband Ryan had been traveling for work during the month of June, so she and her friends decided to go on a girls' trip.

Money was tight for all of them and so they decided to have a staycation of sorts by only traveling to places in their home state of Maryland. Looking out her window now at the rain and leaves, Emma remembered the warmth of the sun as they started their adventure. Ocean City was the first place on their list. Emma smiled as she remembered riding over the Chesapeake Bay Bridge, windows down, music loud, and the summer ahead of them. They stopped just over the bridge at a local tiki bar to enjoy lunch. Emma was happy to just sit and stare at the beautifully calm water with the bridge in the background. Now that she thought about it, Maryland had plenty of water views that were equal or even more amazing. Throughout their trip she and her girlfriends had explored the entire Eastern Shore—the beaches of Ocean City, cruising the Maryland waterways in an old steamboat, out to Smith Island for crabs and their famous Smith Island Cake, St. Michael's for shopping, and revolutionary style history in historic Chestertown. The views in every county they stopped in were breathtaking. Emma hadn't realized until that moment that there was so much about her home state that she didn't know; nevertheless, she was determined to see it all.

Back in her apartment, the rain was finally starting to subside, making Emma hopeful that the Orioles game would not be delayed or canceled. She turned on the TV to find that it had been delayed by two hours. Sighing, she turned it off and went outside. "Guess we'll have to find something else to do until game time," she said to Mugsy, her little terrier. She and her husband lived in Baltimore City and, as huge Orioles fans, missing a game was not an option. She stepped out onto her balcony, the air smelling of fresh rain. "It's so pretty," she said to herself. She truly loved the state of Maryland. Ryan had taken her on a surprise visit over the summer to other parts of the Old-Line State she had never seen before. They'd taken a long weekend to explore Central Maryland including a visit to Glen Echo Park and the famous Dentzel Carousel. What Emma hadn't expected was to find so much history and culture along the way. She learned there was a rich transportation history—railroads in Carroll County and trolleys in Montgomery County. There were natural parks to discover with boating, fishing, and hiking. The views there were stunning and the variety of wildlife surprising.

She and Mugsy walked to their favorite dog park not far from their apartment. When she let him go, he ran with his tongue hanging out of his mouth. He would love to visit the openness of our state parks, she thought, as she watched him run. Maybe they'd move out there one day. Mugsy's running crunched the leaves around them and reminded Emma of the trip she and her mom had taken to Western Maryland late in the summer. It had been dry and leaves were starting to fall in the western counties. Some had even started to turn colors. She and her mom planned to visit all four counties and experience something in each one over the span of four days. As with Central Maryland, it was amazing the amount of rich history and beautiful scenery that awaited them. They started in the town of historic New Market in Frederick. The little town was nestled among the vast rolling hills of northern farmland. Shopping for antiques was a must and the shops in town did not disappoint. Did she really need ten antique books and a 1950s Radio Flyer Wagon that she purchased their first day? No, but after seeing them she couldn't live without them.

The next day, heading west, the two ladies were amazed when they stopped to rest at Sideling Hill in Washington County. They stared at the man-made mountain pass that exposed layers and layers of rock, a geologist's dream. Emma and her mother knew nothing about geology, yet there was something beautiful about the colors hidden inside the mountain. Emma remembered driving through the rest of Western Maryland in awe of the height and beauty the mountainous terrain provided. State parks, forests, and lakes were abundant and ready for she and her mother to explore. As avid hikers, they were in heaven. The last day of their trip they explored the C&O Canal National Historic Park in Garrett County. Emma's mother was very intrigued by the history they learned there because her ancestors had worked the C&O long before.

Rain clouds were forming again as Emma and Mugsy walked home. She looked up at the sky and said, "we better get home fast little pup." They ran up the steps to their apartment building just as the first raindrops fell. At home, Emma walked into her library and pulled out two books she had been given for Christmas last year. They represented both Maryland's military and maritime history, two of her favorite subjects. The small state's historical significance was not lost on Emma; she had studied it extensively in college at St. Mary's College of Maryland. Her love of history took her to many places in Maryland that summer. She had taken a weekend to visit Concord Point Lighthouse, built in 1825 in Havre de Grace, to learn more about its significance during the antebellum period. Looking through her maritime history book, she saw pictures of Solomons Island and remembered fondly a visit to her friend that included a tour of the Calvert Marine Museum where she discovered a wealth of information on fossils and the area's maritime history.

Looking out her library window Emma could see the rain still falling heavier than it was before. She looked at her watch. "I guess the game will be completely canceled now," she said as Mugsy jumped into her lap. Sinking deeper into her oversized chair, she began to read the book she treasured most, A History of Maryland. The book covered the history of her great state from its inception to present day with beautiful pictures spread out through its pages. Emma turned to the pages describing Maryland's birth in Historic St. Mary's City. She had been to the living museum numerous times during her college years. The grounds around the city were quiet with knowledgeable interpreters spread throughout. It was beautiful. Turning the page again, she found a picture of Surratt House in Prince George's County. It was home to Mary Surratt, accused conspirator in the assassination of President Lincoln. Civil War history is prevalent throughout Maryland and Emma had been to Surratt House a couple times to learn as much as she could. She turned the page one more time to find a picture of the Maryland State House in Annapolis. It made her think of her favorite time period in Maryland, the Revolutionary War. Throughout the state it was easy to find areas that had a history with the founding of the United States. Places like Rodgers Tavern in Perryville, where revolutionaries such as George Washington and Thomas Jefferson visited, and small seaport villages such as Port Tobacco in Charles County. Even the State House contributed to the history of the nation as the place where George Washington resigned his military commission.

    Emma stood and stretched. Feeling the need for fresh air, she walked into her room and out onto the balcony, stopping to watch the late afternoon shadows dance over the buildings of Baltimore City. The rain had subsided, making way for a potentially gorgeous sunset. Emma leaned on the railing reliving the memories she had been playing in her mind all day. Maryland was her home and she loved its history, beaches, seafood, mountains, small towns, shopping, waterways, sports, nature, culture, and cities. It was truly a summer well spent. The sound of a distant click coming from the front door pulled Emma from her thoughts. Mugsy barked and ran toward the door. "Emma?" her husband Ryan called. "On the balcony," she answered. A few minutes later he appeared, two cups of coffee in his hand. Putting his arm around her he stared at the sunset and said, "It's a beautiful sunset tonight." She smiled and said, "It is."

MEREDITH JOHNSON is a blogger and first time published author. She holds a B.A. in History from St. Mary's College of Maryland and has several years' experience in blogging and creative writing. She currently lives in Maryland with her husband and two sons.

Autumn Island
By Emmy Nicklin

When Bessa was nine her hair turned gray. Well, to be fair, it was more silver than gray. Some blamed it on the abnormally high tides, others on the dismal blue crab harvest of that year, but most claimed it was the island itself that had turned her hair that vibrant, glinting shade—that it had done so as it slowly slipped into the warm, milky waters of the Chesapeake. You see, the island was sinking.

Bessa didn't mind the silver. In fact, she quite liked it. She brushed her hair ninety-seven strokes a night (the age to which she hoped to live), then tiptoed out to the dock, getting down on her belly to flip the tips of her hair into the water. There they floated, absorbing so entirely the night sky and its reflection in the bay that some would say the moon had come down to the earth that night at the end of Frank's dock.

Frank was Bessa's father. Frank was a worrier and had been ever since the Hurricane of '64 had swallowed up his own father. It had appeared out of nowhere at the tail end of season—a pocket of fierce, tangled thunder and wind in a surprised November sky.

The island had lost a lot of watermen in that storm, and most learned to accept it. So it goes—survivors mumbled over coffee on their front porches or oyster stew at Lorraine's Café. They died doing what they loved—Pastor Stevens reminded them again and again from the pulpit. Still Frank clung to the idea that his father might still be out there, gripping an oyster reef or floating on his back in the salt. Maybe one day he'd rise up out of the water—boots and all—and make his way to Hannigan's, where he'd order the cheapest whiskey and sit quietly on a stool in the corner sipping it.

But then the bay-soaked men started to wash up on shore, including Frank's father with soggy, crab-nibbled limbs, and wide-open eyes. Frank was the one to find him among the marsh periwinkles of Pocomoke Cove, a crumpled, muddy heap in the green reeds.

And so it was only natural that Frank worried about his daughter's silver hair, too. A premature death? Too long in the sun? The fate of a motherless child? What did the silver mean? He worried about her in the morning over his coffee, at dawn on his deadrise as he motored out to check his crab pots, Sunday morning at church in the third pew from the front, at night on a lumpy mattress beneath an open window. Gnawing, crafty, all-consuming worry. But he didn't say a word, just a solid, cupped hand on the back of Bessa's head as she handed him his thermos full of onion soup each morning.

Bessa didn't know, of course. She couldn't guess at her father's delicate nerves. Otherwise, maybe she wouldn't run barefoot across the island in faded, green dresses and hand-me-down jumpers courtesy of the Carters next door. Through yellow marshes at day's end, she ran hard and fast so that the cattails and reeds bruised, bullied, even bloodied her arms and legs. And then out of breath, she arrived at water's edge, chest heaving, leg bleeding, lips smiling.

In April, when the water rose to Ada's front yard (hers was the first house on Main) and didn't recede, they knew it was only a matter of time.

God's got after us some said while others stacked

rocks and dead branches in front of their porches. As the sea rose, so too did the piles of decrepit wood flimsily guarding their homes against the second coming, rising with the brown, murky tides around them.

When tourists mentioned climate change, the islanders smiled an all-knowing smile, shook their heads, and kept their mouths shut until the last ferry of the day moved out and set its bow directly into a boiling yellow-red sun.

Climate change my ass. They knew better.

***

In June, after school lets out from the one-room trailer-turned-schoolhouse, Frank loses yet another first mate to the lure of mainland's terra ferma. And so he approaches neighboring watermen about combining forces—doubling the working hands and number of crab pots (not to mention saving gas). But even his one remaining first cousin on the island refuses.

"Come on now, Frank," Paul says, leaning back in the folding chair on his front porch. "You know there's barely enough crabs out there as it is. I need all them I can get. And Judy—if she found out I be splitting profits—she be through the roof." He spits a black, tar-like substance into an old Coke can that has taken up residence in the corner of the porch. "You know how it goes." He squeezes Frank's shoulder.

In the morning, with no first mate to help, Frank rises earlier than usual. He pulls on his rubber boots, fastens his overalls, and grabs a thermos full of coffee and two tomato sandwiches. He pulls the door closed with a gentle click (trying not to wake sleeping Bessa) and walks in the pre-dawn black down to the dock.

When he reaches his boat, red light is inching its way to the surface of the horizon and the flat, endless water in the east. Still, figures and objects remain fuzzy and ghostlike in the half dark. Then he sees the silver. There asleep on the lines in the stern of the boat, her cheek pressed up against one of the life vests, is Bessa. She's wrapped in his old poncho with her purple rain boots pulled high and silver hair looped into a ponytail. When Frank scoops his arms underneath her back and legs to take her up to the house, she stirs.

"No, Papa." She wiggles down from his arms and starts to untangle and organize the crab pots. "I'm here to help."

"How long you been out here in the dark? Now you know this is no place for a young lady."

"No, Papa, you need me. What are you going to do out there without Jack?" She coils the lines in clean loops the way he had taught her to do. Then she holds up a brown, paper bag. "I packed us lunch—apples and peanut butter crackers. But I forgot the soup."

"You're too little, baby girl. Come on up to the house for some pancakes."

She sits down next to the crab pots and folds her legs firmly across one another. "I'm not leaving." She grabs hold of the nearest cleat for emphasis.

The sun is already halfway up by then and because he's exhausted and already running late, Frank starts the engine. He turns toward Bessa: "Alright then. Drop those lines."

As they motor out, Bessa is strong and quick on the boat. She pulls up pots and darts between lines and wires and nets. She uses her skinny wrists to coax on-the-loose blue crabs out of the tiniest of crevices. But despite her natural ease into this world, Frank still worries. He straps her in a snug life vest and loops a line around her ankle just in case she falls overboard.

By eleven o'clock mid-morning, they break, anchoring for fifteen minutes just south of what is left of the long-abandoned Cedar Island, where a community of one-hundred-and-fifty watermen and families once lived (though not a single Cedar Tree despite its name). The clamor of Frank's diesel engine gives way to gull and geese calls, and there they pause, eat their sandwiches, and imagine (or rather Frank imagines) their own Autumn Island sucked into the sea just like Cedar.

Perhaps it would go quickly, one house falling over another and then another and another, crashing into the bay—loudly, suddenly, but then it would be over. All consumed by brackish waters, all save the church's steeples, rising high and powerful still over the now underwater community. Its docks, its graveyard, its row of sweetbay magnolias lining the post office fence—all of it now swallowed whole by the water.

Or perhaps it would go slow, nearly unnoticeable at first—the crab shacks would seep into the ground, then the water. Gradually the dirt roads on the outskirts of town would become canals. Then the houses themselves would slowly slip away—floorboard by floorboard, beam by beam.

Frank dwells, immersed in these thoughts, but not Bessa. Bessa looks straight up into the sun, then out to the elegant stride of a blue heron. And, when the heat gets too much for her, when dribbles of sweat become layers of wet, uncomfortable skin, she unties the line around her ankle, walks to the edge of the boat, and hurls herself into the water with a shout, overalls still on. Frank creates a stepladder for her out of extra line, but he doesn't end up using it. When Bessa is ready to get out, when her silver hair is soaked through and her burning skin soothed for the time being, Frank reaches over and pulls his daughter out of the bay with one arm scooped around her small back.

***

The night before she left them, Bessa's mother held onto her like that, clinging and grasping all through the dark hours, desperate for some feeling of motherhood and joy for the baby she never wanted. But it wasn't there, and, like her mama always told her you can't force something that isn't there—like the love she no longer felt for Frank and the island, like the milk that was strangely absent from her breasts.

At daybreak, they finalized arrangements at the Walcott Health and Wellness Center in Salisbury. It was not right, and they all knew it—even newborn baby Bessa knew it to some degree. She took the noon ferry on a gorgeous October-blue day, and though she felt relieved on that boat headed north, she wept when she looked back at Frank and baby Bessa in his arms.

When Bessa grew older, the letters started to appear. Frank would present them to her just before supper, holding them out in his palm like a praying mantis—majestic, delicate, important. First it was a postcard from Crisfield—a water tower with a giant red crab painted on top of it. On the back of the card, slanted, loopy letters covered the 4x6 space in four short lines.

Baby Bessa—You darling girl. It's a gray one today, but we expect the sun to show her face this Saturday. I hope it will be bright where you are, too. One day you will know. You will grow big and strong and happy without me. I promise you baby girl. xoxoxo

And soon another from Staunton, Virginia—a picture of low, purple mountains glowing in a Shenandoah sunset:

Baby Bessa—It is cool and quiet up here in the Valley. This is where I grew up with Grandmamma and Papa… did you know that? Out here on the farm, we would pick apples in the fall, onions in the spring, and the sweetest corn in the summertime…sweet just like you. xoxoxo

And another with yellow blocks of all uppercase letters spelling out "Delaware" across a too-blue ocean with white seagulls and superimposed dolphins:

Baby Bessa—Have you ever been to the beach? I don't mean the bay beach…I mean the real beach. A beach on the ocean. The waves are so much bigger here, my girl. I'm afraid I will be washed out to sea so I don't dare go in. Instead I fly a purple kite from the dunes and think of you. Is purple your favorite color, too? xoxoxo

Like that they would come. Short little blurbs from not-so-distant places, always within reach, always with love. Bessa read those postcards cautiously at first, then tucked them under her arm, crawled into her father's lap, and kissed his cheek. She knew the handwriting, recognized the loopy "s"s and "e"s almost immediately as those of Ms. Elaine down at the Grocery. And she began to notice, too, that the postcards happened to come from the same places that the Hoggans or the Carters or the Lees or any of the other island families had recently visited. Still Bessa delighted in these letters and the island love they represented. She saved them, tied them with a blue ribbon, and kept them stacked on her bedside table.

***

Toward summer's end, the crabs are all but disappeared, and Bessa's hair has grown a deeper, lovelier shade of silver. Her moonlit visits to water's edge grow longer and more frequent, too. On nights when it is particularly steamy and sleep is coveted but hard to come by in sticky sheets, Bessa wades into the bay in her nightgown, leans into the warm waves, and floats on her back. She lets her silver hair down from her ponytail to stream long across the surface of the water, and when she does minnows and mummichogs playfully dart in and out of her glowing hair. On nights like these, Frank leans out through his open window, innately worried at first.

But when he stares out at his dock and Bessa swimming beneath it, he is momentarily soothed by the buzzing cicadas in the trees, the purple wildflowers that overrun his yard below, his daughter so naturally, so easily held up in the water.

In the mornings, as crab pots remain empty, most watermen sleep in and take up odd plumbing or handyman jobs. But Frank and Bessa persist. They continue to rise in the morning, pull on their gear, and cast off the lines.

The Friday before Labor Day is unusually gray when they motor east of Autumn Island. It stretches far out in front of them—the gray sky, the gray water. The two blend together so that Bessa thinks for a minute that the world is without end. Here and there, long strips of land and marsh interrupt the gray. So do birds. Lots of birds. Pelicans and seagulls and cormorants and egrets. They fly alongside the deadrise, straight into the wide open.

Frank and Bessa check their pots, no longer expecting to find much, but they pull them up all the same, and stare at the empty cages, strewn with sea grass and bits of barnacle. Then they motor south. Frank goes fast, and Bessa beams, hair in the wind, wind in the face.

At Cedar Island, they sit side by side and eat their lunch. No soup that day—it is too hot for soup, and so they eat cucumber-and-tomato sandwiches on doughy white bread. There are no words between them, but that is not unusual.

And as they stare out at fast-fading Cedar Island that day something is altogether different. No more thoughts of sinking houses and submerged crab shacks—instead, Frank sees something else. There in the center of what is left of the island—where Frank suspects the highest point of land to be—a loblolly pine stands. It is short, green, and young still, but Frank knows it will grow tall. Maybe it will grow old, too, holding together the crumbling, sinking earth a little while longer.

"See that right there, baby girl? Those trees can live to be 300 years."

On the way back in, they check their remaining pots. Bessa leans most of her body over the boat's edge as she pulls up the last buoy's line, wrapped in algae and mud. Fist over fist she pulls, but this pot is heavier than the others. Frank comes over to help, catching the line with his left hand and together they pull the wired cage to the surface.

It looks bare at first like all the others, but then there's something in the bottom left corner of the cage still submerged in the bay. A blue-and-red claw rises above the surface of the water. And can it be? A little glint of silver in it, too?

"Well I'll be."

Frank delicately lifts out the crab. Holding it up into the gray sky, the silver glint is even more obvious. And he forgets his worry for a moment and places the crab firmly but gently between Bessa's two hands. It is riled up, stretching and clawing and pinching the air, but Bessa holds firm, waiting for direction from her father.

"That one goes back in."

She looks up at his stubbled, graying chin while clutching the crab a little longer. And then with both hands, dipped low into the water, she lets go. "Yea, he must have babies to get back to."

***

Florida: Someone once said that it is the state with the prettiest name. I hadn't thought about that before, baby Bessa, that states could have pretty names. Flo-ri-da. Sound it out and let it roll off your tongue. It's beautiful, isn't it? I'm here now and will be for a time. The world is such a big, wide place. It's good to go out there and explore it, my darling girl. xoxoxo

***

The following summer, even after Frank and Bessa move away to the mainland to where the ground is a little more solid and life a little less uncertain, people say they sometimes see her. On those nights when the moon is round and movie-picture big, they think they see the girl with the silver hair lying on a dock with the tips of her hair draped in the water. Or they see her at day's end, out in the yellow meadows, running fast and strong, silver hair streaking behind her.

EMMY NICKLIN lives in Annapolis by way of New York, Key West, and Virginia. She has written for a number of publications, including *Key West Magazine* and *The Piedmont Virginian Magazine*, as well as for environmental organizations The Nature Conservancy and the Chesapeake Bay Foundation, where she currently works. She has a master's in writing from Johns Hopkins University and her fiction has appeared in *The Toast, Delmarva Review,* and *District Lit*.

 By the River

By F. J. Talley

"You don't look so good." The gravely voice scared me. I turned to look at a smallish Black man who looked every bit of seventy-five years old. The man kept looking at me, waiting for an answer.

I looked up and smiled. "I guess so," I said. "Things have been tough."

"Mm hmm." The man joined me sitting on the bank of the river; he didn't care about the dirt any more than I did. Only then did I see his grizzled dog, her tail wagging slowly. I can't say I minded the company, but I came here to be alone. The old man read my mind.

"You look like you want to be alone."

"Kind of."

"Well, this is my river," the man began, "so I'm not going anywhere."

He noticed my reaction, and smiled. "But that doesn't mean you can't stay."

I laughed. "Your river, huh? How did that happen?" The man's face grew even more serious.

"Everybody owns this river, son," he said. "This river and the Potomac are what kept this place alive for hundreds of years."

"No offense," I said.

"Don't sweat it," he said. "You're not the only person who doesn't get it." The man gestured to his dog, who sat by his side. "I'm a waterman, or at least I used to be. Spent my life gathering oysters, like a lot of people around here, especially old people." He looked at me again. "Why don't you tell me your story?"

I hesitated. "It's personal."

"Always is."

"Why not?" I thought. *He's probably the first person who really wanted to know.* "My wife said I wasn't good enough as a father or husband. She took the kids and moved to California – the state, not the town. It was too late for me to follow them, so I had to stay here. And my teaching certificate isn't valid in California, at least not yet."

"Uh huh." The old man said. "And I bet that hurt you a lot. But you don't have to lose yourself at the same time."

I could feel my shoulders sag. "The kids hardly ever talk to me when I call them. It's like I don't exist." It was only then that I looked more carefully at the dog. "Has she always had three legs?"

"Since I've known her."

"I didn't notice before."

"Didn't have to. Doesn't bother her; shouldn't bother you." The man stood. "You ain't no more broken than her, so don't act like it."

* * *

Summer can be hard for teachers. Things have been tough since my wife left, and I've only been able to squeeze in two visits so far to see my kids. I guess I'd forgotten what loneliness was. My principal gave me some leeway, and I've never been happier for the school year to start. At the end of the third week, I drove over the bridge to Solomons to walk the boardwalk and get some ice cream. The old man was sitting in a chair watching the water while his dog drank water.

"How you doin', son?" I sat on the boardwalk by him.

"Not too bad," I said, pointing to the water bowl. "I

never noticed that dog bowl before."

"You don't notice much, do you?" the man asked.

"I guess not."

The man pointed past the railing of the pier. "It's almost time for the sailboat races."

"Races?"

"Yep," he said. "Every Wednesday in the summertime."

Several sailboats were moving gracefully around the water. I couldn't figure out how they were going to get in a line, let alone race. I turned back to the old man. "Did you used to race?"

"Waterman, son," the man said with a dismissive wave. "I didn't have time to play with sailboats." He turned back to the river. "It's a beautiful thing, though."

"Do you have a family?"

"Nope," he said. "Wife and daughter died a long time ago. My son moved away about twenty years ago and never came back."

"Must be a little lonely for you."

The man shrugged and looked up. "It can be tough for anybody if he's alone."

"I guess." I shook myself, then asked, "What do you do when you're,"

"When I'm feeling too alone," he began, "I go to the county fair."

"What?"

"County fair," he repeated. "You know, rides, fatty foods, farm animals – the county fair."

"Seriously?"

He looked at me like I was the densest man he had ever met. "Yep. If you ever want to see people get along together having fun, and nobody does anything bad to anybody else, go to the county fair. I don't ride the rides any more. I hardly ever eat the food. But I watch the people. I look at the kids all proud of their sheep even though I can't stand the smell. I check out all the dresses and jackets and quilts people sewed."

He stretched and looked squarely at me. "You go there and you'll see engineers, farmers, teachers, plumbers, watermen, people who work in little stores, Black folks, White folks; it doesn't matter. Everybody loves the fair. You ever go?

"Once. Last year."

"Did you enjoy it?"

"I don't remember."

"Then try it again."

The man raised his hand. "Shh. The race just started." We watched silently for forty-five minutes, hearing unintelligible shouts from the boats and cheers from the pier. The old man watched like he knew exactly what each boat was going to do. *So that's how it's done*," I thought.

When the races were over, the old man stood and folded his chair. "You remember where the fairgrounds are?"

"I think so."

"Good," he said. "I think the best days are Friday night and Saturday during the day." With that, he and his dog ambled away.

* * *

The schools are closed on the Friday of the county fair, and I really didn't want to run into all my students and their parents then, so I opted for Saturday. I kind of remember this from last year, but just took a slow walk around the grounds, remembering the buildings with the quilts and art work and produce. *I'm not in Kansas anymore, but I could be.* Turning the corner by the food booths, I met the old man and his dog. I frowned.

"How did get your dog in here?"

He looked down quickly before answering me. "I told them she was a therapy dog."

I laughed.

"Who's going to argue with an old man?" he added. "Besides, all the sheriff's deputies know me and know her, and I know all their mothers. They're not going to stop me from doing anything." His eyes had a twinkle I hadn't noticed before.

"How's school?"

"It's been pretty good," I said. "And good to have something to do."

"How about the family?"

I thought for a moment. "I'd say better," I said. "I was able to visit them a second time last month and I don't feel so disconnected. And when I talk to my kids of the phone, they actually talk to me."

"That sounds good," the man said. "Real good."

I looked around at the booths and saw the carnival midway and the rides. "This is kind of an odd gathering of people, isn't it?"

"I suppose you could say that," the old man said. "It's the real America to me. Think about it: there are people here who have almost nothing. Dead end jobs or only part time jobs or between jobs. There are people here who work as hard as they can and barely make it. But they're all here next to doctors and retired admirals and everybody is having a good time."

"What's your point?

"Don't have one. You have to make your own points in life. Now if you haven't see the barnyard pig races, you ought to see them and check out the chainsaw art guys."

"Chainsaw art guys?"

"Don't laugh, it's pretty good to watch. Hard to see how anybody can make art like that, but they do." He turned to walk down the midway.

"Where are you going?"

"To get some fried Oreos."

"I thought you didn't eat fair food anymore?"

"That doesn't apply to one order of fried Oreos."

"Oh."

* * *

One month later, I saw the old man and his dog again at the fairgrounds.

"Surprised to see you here," he said. His dog was right by his side as he sipped down an oyster shooter.

"My school is running a bake sale to raise money for childhood cancer treatments. I took the early shift to help out." I looked down. "Guess I could take off the apron, though."

"Leave it on," said the man. "People respect folks who work at this festival." He smiled. "It looks good on you."

"What should I make sure I do here?" I asked. The man looked behind me.

"You had lunch yet?"

"Nope, I was,"

"Come over here." The man got in a short line, ordered and paid before I knew what was happening. "What do you want to drink?" he asked, pointing to a board.

"Lemonade," I said to the man in the food truck. We picked up our drinks, and the old man took a bag of food and led me to a picnic table. His dog sat at his feet. After giving the dog a small bit of food, he gave me a wrapped package.

I opened the package and found a thick sandwich on white bread. "What is it?"

"A stuff ham sandwich," the man said.

"A what?"

"How long have you lived here?"

"Three years."

"And you've never had a stuffed ham sandwich?"

"No. but what…"

"It's about eating, not talking. Try it." I bit into the thick sandwich, tasting the vegetables and spices. "This is good; a little spicy."

"I'm from Ridge. We put in more pepper flakes there."

"Does everybody make this down here?"

"Mostly old timers," the man said. "But we're keeping it alive." He looked up. "Do you like it?"

"I do," I said. "Just another unique thing from the county, right?"

"Yep." We ate in silence for a while, with each of us giving his dog small bits of ham.

"So three years?"

"Yes," I said. "This is my fourth."

"And how do you feel about Maryland now?"

I smiled. "Do you really want to know?" The man's head tipped. "Right," I said. "You wouldn't have asked me if you didn't want to know."

"I didn't like it when my wife's job took us here," I began. "But I could get certified quickly and it wasn't so bad since we were all together." I looked up. "It got really bad when they left."

"And now?"

"It's okay," I said.

"Just okay?" He was smiling.

"You have to make your own points," I said. "But it's okay and I'm okay."

"Guess that's good enough," the old man said.

* * *

"That must have been good news," the old man said. My phone had rung with a call from my daughter while we were crabbing. *Does everybody use chicken necks for this?*

I couldn't suppress a smile. "Is it that obvious?"

"Is to me."

"At the end of the call, my wife got on." I looked up and the old man's eyebrow raised, since I never much talked to my wife. "It's a weird twist, " I continued. "She told me that the job she chased when she moved to California may move back here."

"How do you feel about that?"

"Good," I said. "I mean, I've got the certification for California now plus applications in to all the districts near where they're living, but I'd just as soon stay here. Here would be easiest for me."

"How about for your kids?"

"Good for them, too," I said. "They're excited about going to our county fair next year." His eyebrow rose again.

"*Our* county fair?"

"Did I say that?"

"Yep." I looked at the river, the old man and the dog.

"Yeah," I said. "I guess I did."

Tropical Storm

By Kevin Lavey

Days before a hurricane hit the Carolinas, he and Margie sat on the couch, laptop propped on his knees, tracking it on the NOAA website. He told her that once it crossed onto land it would go right up the east coast.

"How do you know?" she said.

"I know. I love this stuff."

His wife Margaret crocheted in a chair across from them. She and he had fought last night. In the quiet aftermath, he'd sat on the edge of the bed.

"Dickie told me one more time, I get fired," he'd said. "I won't do what my father did to us. It's over. I'll stop," he said. "You'll see."

"We've got bills, Eugene. Open your eyes. Look at the basket on the desk over there."

"You'll see," he said.

She listened to him talk to their daughter at the computer.

"See here," he said pointing. "These are the Lesser Antilles. Look at that storm there. See? There's the eye of it."

"Where did they get the pictures?" Margie said.

"A reconnaissance craft of some sort."

"A what?"

"Somebody in an airplane flies over and takes them. Maybe it's a satellite. But right here, can you see it?"

"I guess," she said.

"Look," he said. "It came all the way from Africa."

"That's pretty," she said pointing to the multi-colored graphics illustrating its path.

"It's going to roar up the coast." He imitated the sound of a hurricane.

"Eugene, don't exaggerate," Margaret said.

"Exaggerate? There's a hurricane brewing. I'm telling you, right up the coast. Maybe the Chesapeake Bay. Baltimore will get slammed."

"You can tell all of that from a weather report when it's still well off the east coast of the United States?"

"Yes," he said. "How many times have you commented on me and the weather channel?"

"Margie, do me a favor. Go down and take the clothes out of the dryer, would you? Bring the basket up here."

When she heard Margie's footsteps reach the cement floor of the basement, she said to Eugene, "You've been drinking, haven't you?"

"What? I can't believe--"

"I thought you were going to an A.A. meeting tonight."

He started to say something. She lowered her crocheting needles and yarn. "Eugene," she whispered. "I feel old." She lifted her lined face to her husband.

He touched his finger on the spacebar to light up the computer screen again.

The motor that ran him, a sourceless pulsation, silent-echoed through the room, though she could never point to it and say, there it is. That's it right there.

"I didn't get this way on purpose, Eugene. These things happen."

"What are you talking about? I never said a thing about that. Never. Not once."

"Your wife has an operation. They think they got it

all, then she goes in for another one. She has to walk around with a cane. For who knows how long." She shook her head and looked at her yarn box on her lap where her hands rested.

"Last night, I told you I quit. So I quit. I mean, I can't believe you think that I would begin again after I told you." He rubbed his knuckle into his nose. "I would never..."

She picked up her crocheting needles.

He reached down for his cup from a cubby shelf in the coffee table and sipped. He put the cup on the table top then picked it up and sipped again. He quick up-glanced at her. She maintained attention on the crochet needles. Did she subtly shake her head?

Margie arrived upstairs with the laundry basket. She spilled the pile of clothes on the dining room table and began folding. Bruiser, the dog she chose from the SPCA a year ago, had followed her up from the basement. Eugene glanced over to him when he heard his clicking toenails on the wood floor. The dog curled then lay at her feet.

Margaret soft-snapped her fingers to get her husband's attention. He turned to her. She mouthed as quietly as she could. "Your daughter has super sonic hearing. Careful." She pointed a crocheting needle to her ear.

He mouthed back, "Let's enter her in a goddamned contest then."

She tried to stop herself from laughing. He could still make that happen between them.

"You're an ass," she continued to mouth. "A donkey." Her body rumbled with silent laughter. She put her wrist to her eyes to wipe away tears. She inadvertently knocked her cane down from where it was propped against her chair.

At 8:00 a.m. the morning before the storm hit, he climbed onto the roof from Margie's bedroom window and spread a tar-thick sealant at the juncture where the add-on room met the back of the house. Over the past year, water leaked in and stained the dining room ceiling. He pulled lawn furniture inside and remembered to charge the battery unit that would power his daughter's nebulizer in case of a black out. He parked the car away from the London plane trees out front that forever dropped limbs and branches during storms.

He mowed the front and back lawns. The air hung heavy, like a filled wineskin. He sweated through his clothes. His head pounded.

Someone had dumped a bag of shingles and small pieces of wood in a contractor's bag near the mouth of the alley hoping the trashmen would pick it up. He hauled it to the private dumpster next to the apartments knowing that it might burst open in the storm. His neighbor was laid up in the hospital after bypass surgery so he tucked her plants against the house where they would be sheltered by her back steps.

Two doors down, he helped a 70 year old woman remove three elaborate mobile chimes that hung from the roof overhang above her porch. Finished, he decided to knock on doors and ask neighbors, few of whom he knew, if he could secure outdoor furniture or run up to the store for supplies. He helped a guy with a back problem bring a spare folding bed from the basement because his nephew had come to town. Another neighbor, a broad shouldered woman, was lifting slate stones that made a path from sidewalk to her doorway. She said she didn't want them flying like Frisbees around the neighborhood during the storm. They stacked them on a hand-truck then he wheeled them down her basement steps.

At 5:00 p.m. he returned to his house, exhausted,

soaked with sweat, and sat on his front steps like a farmer thinking about his good work, all his good effort that made his life worthwhile.

He could fix it, this goddamned thing that chewed him from inside out. If not, how could he do all that work for everyone? How could he have kept off of it for a full day and get all his chores and duties done?

He listened to the fluttering leaves, feeling the misting rain spray his face. His back ached, his hands throbbed. He felt his heart lift in a joyous celebration of his participation in the world. At last.

He went inside and fell asleep on the couch. An hour later, his wife and daughter came through the backdoor with bags of groceries. They talked about the rain, the dark skies, the crowded store. They came into the living room and tried to rouse him for dinner. He told them he needed to sleep for a while.

"I joined the human race," he whispered to them.

They leaned over him with concerned faces, as if looking for signs of a heart attack.

"Okay," his wife said. "But we need to eat. I'll put leftovers in the refrigerator."

He closed his eyes.

He woke to storm winds lashing the house. His sweat dried clothes smelled putrid. He closed his eyes against the torture of a cottony mouth and a red headache. He stood, stumbled into the kitchen, drank a glass of water, then another. He reached into the bottom drawer of a cabinet and pulled out his pint bottle of Jack Daniels and held it eye level. Moaning with ee-ee-ee sounds through gritted teeth, he dumped the amber liquid down the sink.

Falls Road dropped in elevation near the entrance to I-83. He'd run out of breath from sloshing his way down the middle of the roadway. The noise from the wind in the trees and the whipping rain masked the police car approaching from behind. The officer whooped the siren once. Eugene jumped and turned.

The officer rolled down his window. "You lost?"

"No," he lied. He wanted to laugh.

The officer shined the beam of a flashlight on him and saw a hatless, coatless, soaked man who had been walking down the middle of the road in a tropical storm holding a wrench in his right hand.

"The hell happened to you?"

Eugene turned and sprinted up the hill toward the back of an abandoned two story building. He squirreled through an opening in the fence that bordered the parking lot, and bolted through trees and the thick, unmowed undergrowth of the backlot. He scurried along a ridge that paralleled Falls Road for a hundred yards until stopping at a chain link fence with a high topper of barbed wire. He slid-fell down the bouldered hill until putting feet to Falls Road again. The river had overflowed its banks and spilled out onto the roadway. He waded through fast-moving water mid-shins. The policeman wouldn't be able to drive down here.

He had felt so good about helping his neighbors and tarring the roof and mowing the grass that he wanted to continue his good works. After pouring his liquor down the drain, he grabbed his monkey wrench from his tool box and went into the deluge of rain to the back fence where a loose bolt on the latch of the gate needed tightening.

He couldn't go back in. That no-man lived in there. The guy who fell asleep twice, twice!, when his asthmatic daughter needed to be rushed to the ER. Thank God for neighbors, his wife said. The wife who looked at him like that nearly every day, like she was searching for him.

He went into the alley where water ran like a river, whih he'd never seen before. He could find someone who needed his help, he thought. He walked with his wrench down the middle of Falls Road until the cop whooped behind him and he bolted.

Now, the monsoon of rain came down through the trees and filled the river and water rose and rushed and it pushed him down and rolled him. He held onto the wrench and managed to find his feet again.

He was alive.

"Goddamn," he said. "I'm alive."

He could only see dark shapes within dark shapes in the trees to his right along the banks of the black river. The flow of water above the banks that had spilled onto the sidewalks used by bicyclists and walkers shook and slanted trees, pressed him southward, away from his house. Lightning ballooned the sky.

He should call home. He looked at the monkey wrench in his right hand, and it made him wondrously happy. Yes, he should call home.

He reached in his soaked trousers and pulled out his phone and punched at numbers. It slipped out of his hand and kerplunked into the rushing water. He tried to find it, but it was gone.

He turned and started back toward home in the heavy darkness. What if they needed him? He could help. He could do something.

The flood of river water pushed against him. A wrist sized tree branch banged his leg and sailed past like an unmanned canoe. He looked to the far side of the road. Water had filled the gully and rose above the base of the trees. If he tried crossing to grab a branch, he would be swept away. On the other side was the river. He stayed to the middle of the road. Crazy rumbling sounds liked detonations sounded far away. Rain crackled the leaves.

Homebound, he slogged forward against the stern flow of water. He could make it. He would get to where the road rose above the flooded river and scramble his way north on Falls, go past McClinty's where he'd drunk for the last time in his life. The last time.

The water swelled and he bent lower. Again he looked to the bank, and again he saw that if he went crosswise the water would carry him away. He lowered himself so that his chin rested at water's surface and breast-stroked his arms. He lowered himself farther. He needed a drink. He opened his mouth and drank then choked with laughter. He shouted, "I've drank more than this, you motherfucker."

His feet skidded on the road surface. He pushed off and he tried to swim upstream, but the current turned him and he headed south again in a rush.

He floated fast past a brick building, through the shallow S curve of the road. He swam-walked. The water surged as the road declined. He reached for a branch from a tipped over tree, but the black water carried him toward the dark landscape above the shoreline into a chaos of downed trees and bent telephone poles with their slack power lines.

He pictured his wife and daughter in their upstairs bedroom with a flashlight on between them. They would be lying together, staring at the ceiling.

"What are we going to do with him?" he wanted Margaret to ask their daughter, and herself.

Margie lay on her back with both hands behind her head, ankles crossed, as if on a raft. "I don't know, but he'll be fine," she would wisely respond.

"Let's go down and see if Bruiser is hiding. Point the flashlight over here, will you? I have to find my cane."

He could imagine Margaret lumbering behind her, holding onto the stair railing, still getting used to walking with a cane.

"I'm hungry," Margie said.

"Would you listen to that wind."

Bruiser lay huddled in a corner by the couch with paws tucked against his stomach.

"There's the lights. The power's back on!" Margie said.

Margie fed Bruiser then she and her mother ate bowls of cereal and looked at the back door waiting for him.

"I'm here!" he screamed.

The force of the current tumbled him downstream. He tried to catch foothold on the bottom of the road. He bobbed along. He slammed against the cone-shaped cement base of the train trestle and grabbed at a utility hand grip, losing his wrench. He heaved himself up coughing and hacking, grasped the steel beam of the bridge support, managed to find his feet on a horizontal landing. Wind spun the tops of trees. The flooded Falls River thundered southward like a herd of buffalo.

He screamed, but the rain and rushing water and the tornado of wind whitened his voice into no sound. The water rose above his shoes and he felt the tug of it as he held himself. Again, he screamed for his wife and daughter. "I'm here for God's sake! Look!"

He closed his eyes, leaned against the rusted iron of the support beam. He felt himself both slipping away and holding on as the water rose to his knees in the soundlessness of the roaring storm.

Kevin Lavey is a retired teacher who writes short stories and is working on a novel. He trains in the martial art Aikido.

The Bar on Infinity Street
By Leona Upton Illig

I

"Joe, the fans here in Camden Yards are on their feet and can you blame them? It's been over 30 years since the Baltimore Orioles won the World Series and this stadium is rocking! Do you see that crazy guy in Section 34?"

"Well, Stan, with a 3-0 lead in the top of the ninth and their ace coming out of the bullpen, it looks like they're ready to make history! Listen to the crowd roar as Hernandez makes his way to the mound!"

The three men walked down the cobblestone street and tried to blend in with the crowd. Longshoremen, sailors, and a-rabbers—their horses' hooves striking the roadbed in syncopated rhythm—passed them by. It was getting toward midnight and the throngs of partygoers had thinned. A drunken shout rang out from a back alley but the three men kept moving. They realized, not without relief, that they had attracted little attention. Ed's heavy cloak, and Dash's green tweed suit, had gone largely unnoticed in the darkness. It was true that Harvey's breeches and pink coat had drawn some laughs, but that had been a trifle. The fact was that the humidity pressed down on them more than any strangers' stares. A thunderstorm was on the way.

"Say, fellas, I don't know about you, but walking around out here at night in this heat ain't doing nothing for my creative juices. There's a bar over there. What do you say we go in and have a few? Maybe something will come to us."

"I'm a shade reluctant to chat up the locals, Dash. This isn't Arabia, after all, where I carried letters of introduction. But here, in this place, in this time, I'm afraid it's a bit sticky."

"Listen, Harv, all we gotta do is find a quiet table and sit down. Let me do the talking."

"But a *bar?* It might be a bit dicey, mightn't it? Ed, if you're not completely comfortable with this—"

"Not Hell shall make me fear again. Let us go forth."

"Yes. Quite." Harvey pulled his hat lower over his forehead, and they crossed the street and entered the bar.

It was not hard to find a table in the back. A hanging lantern threw yellow light over it and the chairs. A calico cat, licking its paws, lay on the floor nearby. The men sat down, grateful for the change of air.

The cat got up and moved away.

Harvey was the first to speak. "Sorry to go over this again, but could you read our instructions once more? Perhaps we've overlooked something."

Dash snorted. "Don't I wish!" Nevertheless he pulled an envelope out of his pocket. He glanced around. The bar was empty save for two: a man in a pinstriped suit and a long-haired woman in scarlet. Both seemed engrossed in deep negotiations.

He opened the envelope. "It says here we're supposed to rejuvenate the home team. You know, give them a shot in the arm, and such like. According to this, they've been "dwellin' in the cellar" for a long time, whatever that means. And it says we were picked to help them out because of our Maryland roots and our knowledge of . . . baseball. It's signed by Gabe, but it's got the Big Guy's seal on it, all right. It's legit."

Ed shifted in his chair. His delicate frame suffered from the rough wooden furniture. "It is undeniable that I spent many halcyon days here. But my last night on East Lombard Street was . . . unfortunate."

Harvey grasped his arm. "Try not to dwell on the past, old chap. If only we could have sorted this out in Pleasant Valley! It's so much cooler there this time of year."

"Right. Like strolling around in your nutty animal garden would do us any good. We'd be better off in St. Mary's." Dash took off his hat and smoothed his silver hair. "We could sail over to the Eastern Shore and dive into some of the best hard crabs you ever ate. I can smell 'em now!"

"Ah, the Elysian Shore. As we sail on our pinions—"

"*Eastern,* not Elysian, Ed. *Eastern.*"

Harvey cleared his throat. "Undoubtedly all of us have, may I say, our own Maryland memories. But as for the matter at hand, I'm at a loss."

"You and the rest of us birds, Harv." Dash looked at their companion. "So, Ed, just what are *your* baseball bona fides? Give us something that will make us sit up and bark." He winked at Harvey.

"I expired, ere scarce exalted into birth, shortly after the game's inception."

"Confound it, Ed, you need to look on the bright side of things!" Harvey smacked his riding crop against the table. "Regrettably, I can't say that I was much interested in the sport. But as for my Harford Hounds, well, I could tell you tales—"

"Can it, Harv. We got to stick with the script we came in with. The truth is that none of us knows nothing useful about this game or this team. But we're not leaving here until we come up with something."

"What'll it be, gentlemen?" A waitress, her long hair swept up in an untidy bun, walked over to their table.

Her thin calico dress brushed along the floor.

The three men fell silent.

Ed pulled up his collar.

Harvey looked at Dash.

Dash leaned back and nodded. "Three whiskeys."

The waitress raised her eyebrows. "Sure." A few minutes later she returned with their drinks. She eyed the breeches, the suit, and the cloak. "Just remember, fellas, last call is in an hour. I'll be in the back if you need anything." She drifted away.

Ed stirred in his chair, his dark eyes widening. The cat, which had returned to climb onto his shoulder, stared at the shot glasses. "The sands of time grow dimmer as they run. But, when the proper time arrives, all will come straight in the end."

"He's right," Dash said. "Let's get on with it. We got three good brains here. We can come up with something."

II

"Joe, if I hadn't seen it I wouldn't have believed it!"

"You're right about that, Stan. Hernandez has been overpowering all season! Who'd have thought he'd give up four runs? By all rights the Orioles should be pouring champagne in the dugout right now!

"Well, it ain't over yet, Joe. They can still tie it up with a run and send it into extra innings. Two runs and they can break out the Natty Boh! And the top of the line-up is coming to bat! What a game, Joe! Have you ever seen anything like this?"

The three men had drained their glasses and the smell of whiskey hung over them. Ed sank deeper into his cloak. Harvey toyed with his riding crop, drawing lines on the dusty floor. Dash took out his handkerchief and wiped perspiration off his forehead. With a grunt he brought his fist down on the table.

"We got nothing. We're going to have to go back and tell the Big Guy we blew it."

"That would be a really killing defeat," Harvey replied, *sotto voce*. "These Earth assignments are brutal to get. I overheard one angel say that ever since quantum theory, the Big Fellow has been *extremely* reluctant to authorize field trips. This one's obviously quite important to him." He looked over his shoulder. Except for them, the bar was empty. The man in pinstripes, and the woman in scarlet, had left.

Dash put his handkerchief away. "So I'm listening. Do I hear you giving me any ideas?"

Ed stared straight ahead, as if mesmerized by a specter. "Flee thy lodgings by horror haunted, and homeward turn your soften'd eye."

"I beg your pardon?" Harvey blinked.

"The Naiad airs have brought us home, to the glory that was Greece, and the grandeur that was Rome."

"That's just swell, Ed, but—

Harvey bounced up in his chair. "By heavens, that's it!"

Dash sighed. "So enlighten us, Einstein."

Harvey waved his hand. "Of course we don't know anything about baseball! But what *do* we know? I'll tell you, and here's the ticket—there's no place like home!"

"Okay, Dorothy, so how does that help us?"

"Why, we'll give this team a new home! A brand-new ballpark, full of banners waving in the breeze from foul pole to foul pole! Bleachers and bar stools and busts! Skyboxes and bistros! They'll be positively inspired to win!"

Dash's mouth curved upward. "You may just have something there, Harv. A change of scenery could be just the trick." He looked appreciatively at Ed. "It looks like I owe you one, buddy." He rolled the brim of his felt hat, enjoying its softness. "You know, I always thought you got a bum rap. Me and you—we both deserved better."

Ed's eyes flickered in the yellow light. "Was it not Fate, whose name is also Sorrow?"

Harvey, however, thumped the table in excitement, ignoring his companions. "But where? We haven't got much time left before we have to go back. We can't go traipsing all over the city now, looking for a suitable venue."

"Well, Ed? You know the streets of this burg better than we do." Dash suppressed a grunt in response to Harvey's kick under the table. "Got any more good ideas?"

Ed threw off his cloak and stretched his arms toward the ceiling. "A brighter dwelling place is here for them."

"What, here? Are you *serious?* Why, they'd have to tear this joint down along with most of Conway Street and who knows what else. You really want us to stick our noses in stuff like that? It's bound to tick off the locals."

Harvey waved his crop with renewed vigor. "I, of all people, shall never condone the desecration of antiquities." He glanced around at the bar, eyebrows furrowed. "But, really, friends, look at this place! It's completely run-down—I might almost say, *tawdry*. Just imagine what this area could look like with a gleaming new ball field! Perhaps a tiny garden, with antique roses and fountains, and a topiary or two—"

Ed stood up. "And lo, a stir is in the air! The wave—there is a movement there! Let my heart be still a moment and this mystery explore: 'tis the summer dream—the Idea of Beauty—nothing more!"

"Well, that might be stretching it a bit, but that's the spirit! And we'll give the locals plenty of lead time—say, around a hundred years from now! Their time, of course, not ours! I'd say we've done it, old chaps! We'll tell Gabriel to build a new ballpark right here. It's perfect!"

Dash grinned. "I got to give it to you, fellas. I didn't think we could do it, but we did. Put 'er there!" And the three of them shook hands in a flurry of excitement.

***

The waitress heard the clock strike twelve and left the back room to go out into the bar. "Okay, gentlemen, it's . . ." She stopped. The bar was empty. She walked over to the table with the three drained glasses. On a nearby chair sat the cat, playing with a blank, crumpled piece of paper. "Hey, Herman, can you believe this? They never paid for their drinks! How're we going to make a profit when we get deadbeats like these?"

Her husband came out from the back with a plaid towel folded over his shoulder. He looked around the bar. "Don't you fret, Kate. This time we're gonna make it. I got a feeling things are about to turn around for you, me, the kids, our boy Babe—all of us! Right here at Ruth's Cafe."

III

"Bottom of the ninth, down by one, the Orioles have a runner on third with two out. Hodges is at the plate. Here's the first pitch. A swing and—a miss!"

"Good Lord, Joe. It was right down the middle!"

"The pitcher is stepping off the mound, now he's back. He's on the ropes now. Here's the wind-up and the delivery. It's a curve ball and Hodges fouls it back. Strike two."

"I can't watch, Joe."

"The pitcher has stepped off the mound again. It looks like—what is he doing?—he's tying his shoe. Now he's straightening up. He looks at the runner on third and now he's staring at the catcher. He reaches back,

throws, and Hodges crushes the ball and it's flying out of here and the center fielder is going back, back, BACK TO THE WALL AND HE'S GOT IT!! This game is over! Go to war, Miss Agnes! Can you believe what we just saw? Can you believe it, Stan? Stan? Stan, NOOOOO!"

High above the clouds, in his Private Office, God was sorting through his "Miscellaneous Case Load." Pleased that so many files had been disposed of, he was about ready to take his afternoon nap when he spied a yellow, dog-eared file marked, "Baseball." He smiled and settled back in his chair for a good read. The first item was a synopsis of a recent newspaper clipping.

"Headline: The Oh No O's

"Dateline: October 31

"Story: The Orioles have come close to winning the World Series before, but no loss was more agonizing than their 4-3 humiliation today. How to explain it? Is the curse for real? Scoff if you will, but I'm not! When they razed the Babe's boyhood home at Ruth's Cafe to build Camden Yards, the Orioles' future might have been sealed. When asked about the "Great Losing Spell," as it's known here in Charm City, Manager Dempsey threw his hat down and stomped it into the ground. "Lemme tell you, we're only a couple players away from a championship. Next season we're bringing up a right fielder named Robinson, and a catcher named Palmer, and—"

God sat up. He pressed the intercom. "Bernice, could you get Gabriel in here?"

"Right away, sir."

A few minutes later the door opened and a slim figure in white, wearing wire-rim spectacles, entered the chamber. He tottered up to the desk, an iPad in one hand and a briefcase in the other.

"Have a seat, Gabriel." The Big Guy gestured to the

folder in front of him. "I've just been reading a disturbing report. It says that the Orioles lost the World Series. In seven games. In the bottom of the ninth. After blowing a 3-0 lead." He paused. "Would you care to explain?"

Gabriel's mouth dropped open. "I can't, Sir—I can't imagine what happened!"

"Perhaps I shouldn't have allowed you to run this operation." How long had it been since Gabriel had been assigned this job? He thought back to previous missions. The Edsel. New Coke. Reality TV. His bushy, silver eyebrows lowered in a long, perplexed frown. Delegation did indeed have its downside.

"I'm sorry, Sir, I did exactly as you asked. I found these three fellows from Maryland and I was lucky, they weren't busy or anything, just sitting around reading in the Celestial Library—the old section, you know, not the new wing, nobody ever goes into the new wing—anyway I Googled their names and the words "Maryland" and "sport" and I got tons of hits—so many I couldn't read them all! So I asked my assistants to check them out and the results turned out swell, so I sent these fellows back in time—*really* back in time, to the early 1900s, since it's so hard to smooth out wrinkles in spacetime these days—anyway, they were supposed to come up with something to help the team, and they *did*, they came up with this bang-up idea for a new ballpark in Baltimore and it made everybody *so* happy and—"

The Big Guy raised his hand. "Did you talk to them personally?"

"Uh, no. There wasn't time. I was already working on that rather embarrassing infield incident at the Preakness—I hesitate to bring it up, Sir—You recall that was the summer of—"

"Exactly whom did you pick, Gabriel?"

"Well, you know, there was Ladew, and—"

"Ladew? *Harvey* Ladew?"

"Yes, a tremendous sports hero! He won the title of Master in, uh, I believe it was—"

"Fox hunting. Harvey was a foxhunter. A Master of *Hounds.*" The Big Guy looked at Gabriel, whose nose had begun to twitch in an alarming manner. "Harvey wouldn't know a curve ball from a corked bat. Next?"

Gabriel took a deep breath. "Hammett. He wrote a classic about one of the greatest Oriole players of all time—they even made his book into a movie, and then a radio series! The man was known from coast to coast! He was even invited to address the U.S. Senate!"

God was silent for a moment. "Dashiell Hammett?"

Gabriel brightened. "That's him!"

"He wrote *The Thin Man*. Not *The Iron Man*. Nick Charles, not Cal Ripken. The closest Hammett ever got to sports was sitting in a duck blind on the Chesapeake Bay. With a bottle of bourbon nearby."

The Big Guy had begun to feel tired. With considerable irritation He realized that He would miss his afternoon nap. "Well. So far it seems that you enlisted the expert advice of a fox hunter and a detective novelist. What was wrong with Scott Fitzgerald? Wasn't he available?"

Gabriel blinked and typed rapidly on his iPad. "Sir, it appears that, according to our records, during the time in question, Mr. Fitzgerald—"

"Enough!" The Big Guy bit his tongue. I might as well try stand-up comedy as use sarcasm on an angel, He mused. The heavenly flock was one seriously tough house.

"Relax, Gabe. Where were we? Oh, yes, your last volunteer. And that would be—?"

Gabriel took off his spectacles and exhaled. "No problem with this one, Sir! Why, the entire state named a team in his honor! They *love* this guy! Why, they even built a monument for him—how could anyone go wrong with Edgar Allen Poe and the Ravens?"

LEONA UPTON ILLIG is an author and a book critic. Her short stories have been published by magazines such as *The MacGuffin* and *Sky & Telescope*. Her books, *The Elephant and the Bird Feeder* and *Thumper: Life on the Farm*, were published by 1st Ride Enterprises. A native of Maryland, she lives between Baltimore and Annapolis with her husband and a spaniel named Clara. For more information, please see her website www.threevillagesmedia.wordpress.com.

Welcome Homesick
By Rissa Miller

Cold air blasted through the vintage revolving door of David's hotel lobby. He fidgeted, pulling his jacket around him, and glanced at his phone. The temperature was 44 degrees. San Diego weather was very different, and he was no longer used to the cruel winters of his Maryland hometown.

Seeing Andria hadn't been part of his plans when he came home to interview for the new job. But he couldn't resist. When they offered the first interview, he'd reached out to her on Facebook. She was open to reconnecting. Her face on the computer screen, images of the woman David knew since his early twenties, but who was always out of reach. He had been firmly in the just-friends category as Andria was his roommate Juan's girlfriend, then wife. Despite a move to the West Coast, David never forgot her.

This woman must be crazy. It's freezing out.

The lobby of Embassy Suites on St. Paul Place was an elegant blend of the historic building and chic new Baltimore. Maybe he could convince Andria to sit and have coffee?

He ran his hands down his thighs. If only I had packed jeans. He hadn't foreseen checking out Andria's recently acquired BMW R nineT Scrambler motorcycle. On the phone, he wasn't even sure what she was talking about. To him Scrambler sounded like breakfast. While she explained that the bike was made for street riding but could also handle dirt trails, he searched for it on his laptop. Her shiny toy was a new model but looked vintage, with retro styling and a powerful engine. Everything about it seemed impressive. Andria had certainly upgraded from her old Honda with the loose drive chain.

David sighed and leaned against the large hotel window, picturing the day Andria rode into his life. Her trim curves were clad in a black leather jacket, ripped blue jeans, and tall black boots. It wasn't quite like a movie scene when she pulled the helmet off. Her black hair was stuck in chunks to her head and there were marks on her cheeks from the cheek pads in the helmet. That day was more than a decade past, but he remembered it clearly.

Juan was a good match for her. He quickly got his own bike. More times than David could remember, he watched Andria and his roommate ride off together. He assumed they would stay together forever. It never stopped him from daydreaming though. Likely today wasn't going to be any different.

David had never seen the streets of Baltimore from the back of a motorcycle. She said it would be a blast. When he thought of motorcycles, he worried, imagined the sidewalk and his skin getting too close for comfort.

He heard her before he saw her. The BMW had a cultivated rumble, a sound that hinted at expertly restrained power just beneath the surface. That sound - motorcycle engine. Every time he heard it, he'd turn and look, thinking of her, as if for some reason Andria would be riding in southern California. It made no sense, but still, he had looked for her. And now, she was rolling into the hotel valet lane.

The bike came to a stop, more impressive in real life than it appeared online, and the rider swung off, her back to him as she flipped open the face shield and started taking a bag off the back of the bike. A helmet for him, he knew.

He wanted to see her face, the quick eyes, bold cheekbones, skin flushed pink in the morning cold. Even more he wanted to hear her laugh. Not the dumb "lol" from their recent texts. Andria's laugh, the sound that used to make his heart flip flop. The way it made her nose crinkle and squint those pretty hazel eyes.

It wasn't going to happen in the hotel lobby. David braced himself for the chilly morning and stepped into the reliving door, bracing for the winter chill.

"Hey," he offered, his breath clouding the cool morning air.

Before he could get a good look at her, Andria had spun around and grabbed him in a hug. He felt her arms around his ribs as the hard plastic of her helmet pressed against his chest. Could she hear his heart beating? It must be as loud as her bike.

"David! My God, it's been too long!" Andria said. Her voice was light, she was slightly breathless.

She stepped back with a tiny laugh. Every detail of her had somehow gotten... better. A few lines crossed her forehead and the skin under her eyes. The flecks of green and gold in her irises shimmered in the brilliance of morning sunlight and her wide, engaging smile was the welcome home he longed for in the deepest recesses of his heart.

They briefly exchanged hellos then she pulled a plain black helmet with a face shield from the bag.

"It's colder than I expected, but we'll be okay," she nodded and handed him the helmet. "Here, I hope it fits."

Glancing quickly over Andria's attire, David felt inappropriately dressed. She wore fitted pants, her customary tall black boots, a thick jacket with stiff padding on the arms and shoulders and gloves she might have stolen from a sci-fi movie. He wore business casual pants with a fleece hoodie layered over a tee shirt, regular winter jacket, and his running shoes.

Accepting the helmet, he pulled it on. It was surprisingly heavy and tight, squishing his cheeks until he looked like a fish. Who usually wears this helmet?

"That looks good," Andria said.

His range of vision felt narrow. How does she wear these things all the time?

"Can you fasten the chin strap, or do you want me to help you?" she asked.

"Oh, right," David said, pushing his concerns aside. His numbing fingers fumbled over the nylon strap. He felt along the bottom of the helmet but found no way to fasten it.

"Let me," she spoke after a moment, pulling off her gloves.

Her slightly chilled fingertips expertly adjusted the strap, snapping it into place. The brush of her touch on his neck surprised him. He wished for more.

As he flipped the face shield up, Andria reached into her bag and offered him gloves similar to her own. Men's gloves. No doubt these belong to someone that belong to Andria? She hadn't said so, but he figured she must have a boyfriend. Women like Andria didn't remain single.

"So, tell me about the job interview. Did it go well?" she said as they both pulled on their gloves.

"Oh, yeah, they made me an offer," David said.

The gloves were stiff, hard to move his hands in. But he was grateful for the protection and warmth they promised.

"Congratulations! So…?" He could see her smiling through the clear face shield of her helmet.

"So, I'm coming back," he replied.

It was the first time he'd said it. Even to himself. It

was a huge step up professionally and a long-desired move across the country back to his home state. His remaining family was only 45 minutes from Baltimore in Annapolis. Here, too, was the girl that got away - right here in Baltimore.

Andria gave a tiny hop and clapped her hands together.

"Oh David, that's wonderful! I'm so glad!" she hugged him again. "When will you be coming? Can I help you move or find a new place?"

He shrugged and grinned, no longer able to hold back the happiness welling inside him.

Seeing Andria, he remembered the Baltimore of his past. Old Bay sprinkled across French fries with vinegar and bags of hot peanuts at Orioles games. Nights drinking Natty Boh till dawn, watching Andria and Juan tinker with their bikes. He was ready to return. It didn't matter if she had a boyfriend, he could be happy as just-friends. Andria meant home.

"Anyplace you want to go?" she asked.

David hated to admit it, but he missed all of his city, every inch. The brick townhouses, the rutted streets, the pigeons lined up on ornate historic buildings. One area came to mind.

"It sounds touristy, but can we go by Inner Harbor and Fells Point?"

"Definitely," she replied. "You know, it's changed a lot since you were here."

Andria smoothly swung her leg over her BMW. She was natural on the bike; David knew he would be clumsier. Hopefully his lack of experience didn't cause her any problems riding. As she clicked the kickstand up, she gestured for him to climb on behind her. She was in complete control, despite how the massive machine effortlessly balanced between her legs dwarfed her petite frame.

With trepidation, David approached the BMW Scrambler and climbed up on back of the bike. It swayed for a moment, but he felt Andria steady it, sure and confident.

"You've done this before? Rode with someone on the back?" he asked.

"A million times. Just hold onto me," she replied.

David glanced down. The asphalt was right there. He softly rested his hands on her waist, not knowing a way to touch her that wasn't awkward. It would be awful if she thought he was trying to grab a quick feel, but he wasn't sure how to hold on.

"Hold onto my waist," she instructed firmly. "Really hold on, don't be shy. It's important. You'll catch on quickly, it's like a bicycle, your body will know which way to shift your weight as we turn."

David tightened his grip on Andria's torso. He closed his eyes for a second and took in the growl of the engine, the sensation of the woman in front of him, an awareness of the moment. He felt the bike ease forward and as fast as that, they were out of the valet lane.

The hotel facade whipped by and they turned onto St. Paul, a main thoroughfare heading south towards the harbor. The city passed him in a tactile way, as real as if could touch the buildings, street, sidewalks. Cars created a wall, he understood that now. Cars have doors and windows to lock you in and the world out. On the back of Andria's bike, Baltimore was tangible, closer. And colder. His coat and hoodie were no match for the velocity of 44-degree air steaming across his body as his garments flapped against him.

After a few minutes, Baltimore's Inner Harbor spread out before them. The green-roofed shopping pavilions, the Aquarium. The USS Constellation reached high into the clear blue sky, only to be overshadowed by Baltimore's World Trade Center and several buildings he didn't recognize connected to the Aquarium. Privately owned boats bobbed in the distance and as they stopped at a light on Pratt Street, he smelled the air. It was a mix of city and sea and earthy funk that only could mean home.

David kept a tight grip on Andria as they turned down President Street and what he remembered as a warehouse district came into view as a grouping of chic modern skyscrapers with offices, apartments, and storefronts. This happened while he was gone, a neighborhood reborn between Little Italy and Fells Point.

By the time they were riding down Broadway in Fells Point, David knew Andria was an expert motorcyclist. He let the tension roll off him and simply took in the new places in Fells he did not recognize and smiled at old favorites like Bertha's as they passed. She pulled into a space in front of The Daily Grind, an eternal coffee shop he'd patronized in another life. When she put her feet down, he slid off the left side of the bike.

"I need some coffee, how about you?" she asked.

"That was freaking amazing, Andria," David said. "Seeing the city like that. Why didn't I ever go with you before?"

She laughed as she unstrapped her helmet.

"Good question. You could have," she shrugged.

David turned and looked across the cobblestones of Thames Street to the Harbor.

"Mind if we sit outside? I haven't seen this in years," he asked.

"You know what, just go sit on the dock. I'll be right there," Andria hurried into the coffee shop. David had the urge to follow her, but the siren song of the water overpowered him. Baltimore Harbor was the ultimate symbol of home to him.

Sunshine warmed the morning air as he wandered to

the gray wood planks of the Fells Point dock and sat on a bench. It was a vista he had taken for granted, saying it was for tourist photo ops. Now he pulled his phone from his pocket and snapped several pictures of the Harbor.

"Nice view?"

Andria's voice came from behind him and following an impulse, he took her photo, historic Fells Point behind her. Very nice view.

"Coffee. Perfect, thanks," he zipped his phone back into his jacket and accepted the cup.

She sat beside him, her helmet and backpack hanging from her arm.

"You always loved these," she pulled a container of Berger Cookies from her backpack. "You're not gluten free or something now, are you? I didn't even think to ask."

David couldn't contain his smile as he accepted the box. He loved Berger Cookies. Soft shortbread with hand-dipped thick chocolate fudge topping. It had been years since he had one. His current home in southern California offered no such thing.

"Andria, this is amazing. You have no idea how much I missed these," he said.

"Let's open 'em up," she popped the lid from her cup and sipped her coffee.

He tore the plastic wrapper and the sweet chocolate scent of Berger Cookie melded with the bitter aromatic coffee. Andrea accepted a cookie from the box and gazed over the water.

As he bit into the tender cookie, crumbs of vanilla mixing with gooey cocoa frosting, David considered where in Baltimore he wanted to live. His city had grown up. Baltimore was different, yet with all the new buildings and polish, he felt sure its gritty tell-tale heart was beating the same as ever below the veneer. First, he would accept the offer of Director of Marketing for a well-known athletic wear company. More of a step up than he'd imagined before age 40. Then, he'd pack up and come home. Maybe stay with his family in Annapolis for a few weeks and commute before deciding where to live in Baltimore. He wanted this view, though. The Harbor. The iconic city skyline. Andria and Berger Cookies were a bonus.

"Remember when Domino Sugar caught fire?" Andria asked.

David followed her gaze to the iconic building.

"Yep. We were at your apartment baking… what was it?"

"A peach cake. I wanted to make a peach cake for Juan's birthday," she laughed. "The cake and the explosion at Domino Sugar were kind of, you know, symbolic."

Neither of them knew much about cooking back then, and less about baking. Their peaches were from cans and when there wasn't enough sugar, he had suggested adding more baking soda. When they heard the explosion at Domino, they forgot the cake in the oven. It was a scorched peach glob in the end and Juan never got his peachy treat.

"Ever try making peach cake again?" he asked.

"Yeah, I did. And I can make a really tasty peach cake. You'll have to try it yourself, though," she glanced over and reached for another Berger Cookie.

She's flirting with me.

"I'd love that," he replied. "Say when and where."

"We live in Hampden. Bought a house there a few years back. It has a garage, so I can store my bikes," she said.

Shit. Maybe that wasn't flirting. I'm reading too much into this. May as well hear it. Of course, she lives with a boyfriend.

"Who's we?" he asked.

"Me and my dog Vincent, and our sometimes-cat Pumpkin," she said easily.

David tried not to react. Vincent is a dog, not a boyfriend.

"What's a sometimes-cat?"

"She lives outside. Comes and goes but I feed her and take her to the vet. Occasionally she comes inside to sleep or stay warm. Sort of a step above a neighborhood cat," Andria said.

A water taxi glided into view, taking commuters and tourists to the other side of the harbor. He remembered using them many times on family trips to the Aquarium or for Orioles games. The water taxis also stopped in front of the building where he was going to work. An area of Baltimore just south of Inner Harbor that wasn't even developed when he left.

It was a visible change, like the few gray strands in Andria's straight black hair that had broken loose and flitted around her face. He wished he had stayed in touch with her more. When he left there was a sense that getting away from her and Juan would be good for him. Always on the outside of a happy couple, he felt heartbroken and conflicted by loving them both. He'd been confident San Diego would be different, and there had been girlfriends, one he lived with three years and considered marrying. In the end, none of the relationships sparkled. Never for more than a few months, anyhow. He wanted what he'd seen and known existed once between his two friends. His gamble on a big move ended in loneliness he combatted with long hours at work and focus on a now-successful career.

"This is none of my business… I probably shouldn't ask. What happened with you and Juan? I thought you two would never split up," he asked hesitantly.

"Oh, well, we're still friends," she said and studied the building across from the bench. "Maybe friendly is a better word. We're friendly. Mostly, I wanted to live one life and he wanted another. He's remarried you know, has two adorable kids. We cross paths sometimes. He's very happy and I'm happy for him."

"He and I lost touch after you guys got married," David said.

She laughed.

"I know, I was there. He missed you a lot. I'm surprised he never reached out. I don't know why he didn't."

"How are you doing? You're okay with, like — "

"Oh, it's been several years, David. Yes, I'm totally fine. Life goes on. I love my job in the motorcycle industry and have a close circle of friends. My world is good," she nodded. "How about you? How are you?"

David hesitated and took a long sip from his coffee. How am I? In limbo? Optimistic?

"Homesick. I'm homesick," he replied as realized just how much it was true.

Andria's eyes locked on his for what felt like a long time before she stood up and finished her coffee in one swig.

"No special girl back in San Diego who will move out with you?" she asked.

"No special anything in Cali. Not even a fish. I'm ready to come home," he said.

She nodded. "I need to get you back. Gotta get ready for work and walk Vincent."

Following her lead, he drank the rest of his coffee quickly, put the Berger Cookies back in her backpack and they trekked across the Fells Point cobblestones back to her motorcycle. As he pulled on the helmet, he felt a new reverence for the machine. Nothing about riding with Andria ended up frightening him. He got on behind her and this time, welcomed the rumble of the engine as he wrapped his arms around her.

Andria didn't ride by the water going back to Embassy Suites. She took a faster route through the city, but he didn't mind. The buildings were long lost friends, snapshots from the life he left behind. The blocks passed quickly and before he knew it, he was sliding off her bike and returning the helmet.

They said their goodbyes and David silently hoped it was the first of many times he would see her.

"Hey!" Andria called out.

David heard footsteps behind him and turned to see Andria jogging over with her helmet in one hand and the Berger Cookies in another.

"Did you want these?" she held out the cookies.

"Oh my God, yes, absolutely," he took the box, embarrassed he had forgotten her gift. "I'm sorry — "

"Do you want this?" she asked, quickly leaning in and kissing him lightly on the mouth.

David caught his breath. Did that just happen? Am I dreaming?

"I… yes, I absolutely want that," he stammered.

A playful expression sparkled across her face and Andria winked at him. She pulled her helmet on and turned to go, speaking over her shoulder.

"I'll see you soon. Welcome back, Homesick."

RISSA MILLER studied writing at New York University/Tisch School of the Arts and photojournalism at Western Kentucky University. She has worked for five publications, including *The Baltimore Sun*. She is now Senior Editor at the *Vegetarian Journal* and her latest published work is *Goodnight, Poet*.

Love Among the Black-eyed Susans
By Beth Smith

Whenever I pick Black-eyed Susans from my flower garden, I think back to the summer of 1958 and smile. Just turning thirteen, I was trembling on the brink of adolescence in that less complicated time. Life was slower and more innocent, but still somewhat confusing and concerning to a curious teenager. That summer of 1958, while secretly observing the intricacies of love, sex, and passion, I learned things that left me dismayed and questioning. Most of all, and most importantly, I learned that people sometimes wear masks…

"I have the most delicious gossip," whispered Pamela Sue Burke as we walked under the shade trees on our way home from church.

We skipped right through a large puddle left over from last night's thunder storm, letting the dark, muddy water splash over our sandals. It was just noon, but the sultry air was heavy with humidity. I felt as limp and sticky as Kool-Aid on Mama's dishrag.

"I wish I was at the beach," I said. "July in Maryland is almost like Florida." Of course, I have never been to Florida, but saying that made me feel world-traveled and sophisticated, something I have been trying to be since turning thirteen.

"And," I added, feeling morally superior to my best

and closest friend, "nice people don't gossip."

"Well, it concerns your very precious Mrs. Linda Denton Pierce, miss teenage America," she continued. Pamela Sue couldn't stand that I was a teenager and she wasn't until November.

"I don't want to hear any gossip about Mrs. Pierce, and, anyway, you are just jealous because I weed Mr. Pierce's flowerbeds and he pays me."

"Well, I know something really interesting, and you are just afraid to listen," she said.

I really shouldn't have let her rattle on. She didn't like the Pierces when they moved here, and she still didn't like them. She said they were stuck-up and snobby, and Mrs. Pierce was always hanging on to Mr. Pierce's arm and whispering in his ear.

Pamela Sue hated that. She said her parents knew where and when, and I guess they did. They had six children.

I liked the Pierces. They moved from the city to our town and were fixing up the old Johnson farm. They were quiet and reserved. They were a lot like Mama and Daddy, only they were years younger and tons richer.

They had worked a lot on their house, and it already looked like something in one of Mama's magazines like Better Homes and Gardens. The living room was dreamy and had a grand piano. No one in Lutherville had a grand piano.

Mr. Pierce, to everyone's surprise, joined the local garden club, and within two years, he had won the blue ribbon for the best wildflower garden in the county. Just because he didn't play on the church softball team didn't make him a sissy, even though Pamela Sue thought he was.

In fact, my daddy told me that Mr. Pierce was a very famous war hero and even knew President Eisenhower.

Now he was going to write a book and tell all these amazing things about battles and famous generals. My daddy said Mr. Pierce graduated from West Point and might even run for Congress one day. He was so handsome. He looked just like Gregory Peck, and he was very polite, always saying "good morning" to everyone on Sunday morning.

Mrs. Pierce was dainty and delicate and the most refined lady I knew. She served on the flower committee at church, cut up the bread for communion, and volunteered at the nursing home, and she didn't even have a relative there. She was beautiful, with perfect makeup and blond hair pulled back all neat and nice in a French twist. I thought she looked a lot like Grace Kelly before she went off and married that prince. Mrs. Pierce called Mr. Pierce "dear" and "darling, not "hon" like lots of people do in our town.

Pamela Sue had been quiet while I was ruminating in my head about the Pierces, but I knew she was about to burst.

"I just have to tell you this," said Pamela Sue, putting her head down real close to my ear, "Mrs. Linda Denton Pierce sunbathes without any clothes on at all, right on the grass near the big bed of Black-eyed Susans in Mr. Pierce's garden."

I stopped walking. That piece of news did surprise me some; no one in our town would ever sunbathe without wearing a bathing suit, not even Maggie Burke, Pamela Sue's older sister, who everyone says is the wildest girl in town.

Maggie was supposed to marry Albert Dudley Morehouse, the richest boy in four counties, right after high school. But instead she enrolled herself in a business college in Baltimore, for which, my Mama said the Morehouse family would be eternally grateful.

"I don't believe you, why I've been at the Pierce's farm all summer and I've never seen such a thing," I said, forgetting Maggie for a minute and thinking of Mrs. Pierce in her navy suit and white gloves, a little straw hat perched on her head. She was the most dignified person in church.

"Well, you're only at the farm in the morning, so you don't know everything," said Pamela Sue. "I heard my Aunt Alma tell my mama yesterday when she stopped by for a glass of mama's special sweet tea. Aunt Alma works for Dr. Patterson, and she said Mrs. Pierce came for an office visit a few weeks ago because she had a terrible sunburn."

"She said," Pamela Sue continued in her best I am so smart voice, "she heard Mrs. Pierce tell Dr. Patterson that she sunbathes nude – she actually used the word nude – when no one is around. But she fell asleep near the big Black-eyed Susan flower beds and got scorched. Dr. Patterson was shocked. Aunt Alma said Dr. Patterson lectured her about sunbathing without wearing a swimsuit. Mrs. Pierce said she would consider his advice."

Yikes!

"Maybe she was wearing a teeny, tiny bikini like the one your sister wears," I said, feeling the necessity to defend Mrs. Pierce.

Maggie caused a near scandal when she wore her bikini to the swim club last summer. Maggie says bikinis are all rage in Europe and the more sophisticated places like Miami, her favorite place to mention since her Uncle Harley lives right on the beach in one of the tall hotel buildings. Maggie is very impressed with Miami.

"I have an idea," said Pamela Sue. "Mrs. Pierce invited you to lunch tomorrow, and she said you could bring a friend, right?"

"Yes."

"So, you take me and right after lunch, we say goodbye and then we pretend to leave but instead we hide in the pump house and spy. Maybe, Mrs. Pierce will take a sunbath."

I should have said no right then, but I must admit I was a tiny bit curious. I knew Mama and Daddy wouldn't like me spying, but this might be interesting.

"Ok, I agree reluctantly but if she is wearing a bathing suit, you don't gossip the rest of the summer," I said.

"I won't," said Pamela Sue, triumphantly. "Cross my heart and hope to die." Pamela Sue is always so dramatic.

The next day was hot and sunny. We arrived at the Pierce's for lunch. It was very stylish. We sat on white wicker chairs around a glass-top table on the side porch.

Mrs. Pierce served us tiny sandwiches, cold potato soup in thin china cups, and minted iced tea in glasses with stems. Mr. Pierce, sipping on something that looked like ginger ale, talked all about his blue-ribbon wildflowers. He was especially fond of the Black-eyed Susans.

"You know some people think the Black-eyed Susan is nothing but a weed that grows everywhere," he said in a soft voice that hinted at a southern accent. "But I think it is a noble blossom, Rudbeckia hirta…the symbol of justice…a flower native to our great country…the Indians used it to ward off illness and heal snakebites... bees and butterflies find the blooms intoxicating…he sipped again "Of course, you know it is the state flower of Maryland."

We both nodded, although I think Pamela Sue was getting bored.

After a delicious dip of ice cream smothered in chocolate sauce, we said thank you and goodbye. Mr. Pierce said he was going into the city for a few hours to meet with his book agent. Mrs. Pierce said she thought she would take a nap or maybe a sunbath. Pamela Sue shot me a glance.

In a few minutes, Mr. Pierce drove off in his brand-new Ford station wagon. Mrs. Pierce gave each of us a bouquet of Black-eyed Susans to give our mamas. I felt a little guilty taking them when I knew we were about to spy, but Pamela Sue said, "so what."

We started to walk down the lane, but when we heard Mrs. Pierce go back into the house, we climbed over the fence, circled down by the stream, and cut through the pasture to the pump house. We had hardly gotten our bearings in the damp, cool building when we heard the porch door slam. Pamela Sue scooted over to the louvered window and motioned for me.

Mrs. Piece had changed into a long white robe. She was carrying a big towel and a portable radio. She walked down the hill to the wildflower garden and over to a grassy patch that separated two huge clumps of Black-eyed Susans. She spread out her towel, turned on the radio, shook her hair free, and dropped her robe.

She was stark-raving naked!

Yikes!

I gasped and Pamela Sue, grinning like a Cheshire cat, kept poking me in the ribs with her elbow.

"I knew it, I knew it," she whispered. "She is totally, really totally naked."

I sat down on the cold cement floor and tried to regain my composure.

Suddenly, Pamela motioned for me to come back to the window. "Who is that," she asked, pointing to a someone standing on the hill above the garden.

I peeked through the louvers. "That's Joe Gibbons," I whispered. "He is helping Mr. Pierce rebuild the barn this summer.

"You mean the Joe Gibbons who is dating my sister

Maggie?" Pamela Sue whispered back. "The Joe Gibbons who plays quarterback for Maryland?"

"Yes, and I had better warn him that Mrs. Pierce is sunbathing in the wildflower garden," I said as I started for the pump-house door.

Suddenly, Pamela Sue grabbed me by the cuff of my shorts and pulled me down with a thud. "Oh my God," she said pressing her nose hard against the louvers. "Look."

I knew I shouldn't move an inch, but something propelled me toward the window. I looked out and saw Joe Gibbons, muscles bulging in a white t-shirt and tight jeans, strut right down the hill and into the wildflower garden.

Mrs. Pierce bolted upright, and I just knew she would scream any minute. But she didn't scream; she held up her arms, grabbed Joe Gibbons by his black leather tool belt, and pulled him right down between those two big clumps of Black-eyed Susans. I almost fainted.

"I can't see them," said Pamela Sue, pressing her nose harder against the louvers, "but, wait, a white t-shirt just landed on one of Mr. Pierce's prize-winning Black-eyed Susans."

Yikes. I was scared to death. Even Pamela Sue looked a bit nervous.

"Let's get out of here," she whispered, reaching for her bouquet of Black-eyed Susans. I picked up mine and crawled over to the pump house door, Quietly, we pushed open the door. We could hear Mrs. Pierce laughing. She seemed to be enjoying herself.

Yikes!

We ran all the way home. Before Pamela Sue left me at my kitchen door, we took a sacred oath that we would never, ever, under any circumstances, divulge what went on in that wildflower garden.

That night I was more quiet than usual at dinner.

"Are you ok, Bethie?" Mama asked as she flicked her hand across my forehead. "You don't feel like you have a fever."

"You do look a little pink," said Daddy, ruffling my hair.

"I think I might be getting a summer flu, Mama" I said, as the thought of Joe Gibbons hugging a bare Mrs. Linda Denton Pierce caused my cheeks to suddenly blush up even more and burn very hot.

"Good God," said Daddy, "now she is as red as a raspberry."

"Run upstairs," Mama said gently. "Take a cool bath, put on your shorty pajamas, and I will come up in a minute to take your temperature."

Of course, I didn't have a fever, but I looked so pathetic that Mama said she would bring me an orange popsicle.

As night came, I just couldn't stop thinking about Mrs. Pierce and Joe Gibbons. I closed my eyes real tight and tried hard to get to sleep, but I kept thinking about what Mrs. Pierce and Joe Gibbons must have been doing down in Mr. Pierce's wildflower garden. They were committing a mortal sin! I thought it was humiliating.

I guess Mrs. Pierce and Joe Gibbons had an attack of all-consuming passion. Pamela Sue and I had read about all consuming passion in one of Maggie's paperbacks that she hides under her bed. But all-consuming passion was for exciting people in far off romantic places like India or New York City, not in Lutherville, Maryland.

I am sure Mama and Daddy never had all-consuming passion, and not even the Burkes. Course I know about sex and having babies. Pamela Sue had told me all the details, although she wasn't sure about the naked part. All-consuming passion is something else.

I definitely know about falling in love and feeling all light and airy. A few nights ago, when we were playing hide and seek with the little kids, I ended up with Billy Burke, Pamela Sue's fifteen-year-old brother, under the lilac bush.

I liked being under the lilac bush with Billy. The air smelled so sweet and earthy and the starlight shone right through the branches and danced all around Billy's head, his blond hair almost turning white in the moonglow. He looked so cute, just like Tab Hunter. I was wishing so hard he would lean over and kiss me, but he didn't. He just tweaked my ponytail and ran off. I liked being close to Billy, but never in my wildest dream could I imagine being naked with him.

People don't go around being naked in Lutherville unless they are in the bathtub or Dr. Patterson's office.

Well, once when I was spending the night with Pamela Sue, she talked me into sneaking out of the house and going swimming in the duck pond in our underpants. The water felt so cool and nice, and we were having so much fun when Miss Emily Turner, Pamela Sue's neighbor, turned on her back-porch light and caught us. She called our parents right away and the next day, Pamela Sue and I had to write apology letters to Miss Emily for, what Daddy called, "upsetting her constitution."

Thoughts of nakedness and all-consuming passion were making me restless. I climbed out of bed and headed downstairs to visit with Mama. I heard her talking to Daddy on the front porch, and I was about to open the door when I suddenly stopped and peeked through the screen.

Mama was arranging the Black-eyed Susans in her favorite milk-glass vase. Daddy was stretched out on the porch swing all lazy-like when he suddenly got up and walked over to Mama, brushed her hair away, and kissed her on the neck. Mama turned around and, I could hardly believe this, Daddy kissed her again like I've never seen him kiss her before. It was like William Holden kissing Kim Novak in the movie Picnic.

"Johnny," Mama whispered, "what will the neighbors think?"

Yikes.

I never heard Mama call Daddy, "Johnny." She always called him John.

"Turn off that damn light and come with me." Daddy's voice sounded sort of gravelly as he reached down and took her hand. "Bethie is in bed, the night is young, the breeze is warm, and I want to make love to you."

Yikes.

I ran back upstairs, opened my closet door, grabbed all my used dolls and stuffed animals, threw them on my bed, and jumped into the middle of them. People seems to be acting very strange. I wondered if the Black-eyed Susans were intoxicating them like Mr. Pierce said the Black-eyed Susans intoxicate bees and butterflies.

The next Sunday in church, Pamela Sue and I were cooling ourselves with cardboard fans donated by Wilson's Funeral Home when Mr. and Mrs. Pierce came walking down the aisle. Mrs. Pierce was wearing her navy suit and little straw hat. She smiled at us but ignored Joe Gibbons who was sitting with Maggie in the next pew. Then she put her hand on Mr. Pierce's arm and looked up at him with great big cow eyes. I thought I was going to throw up.

Pamela Sue pointed to the Bible verse on her fan. It read, "Beware of false prophets which come to you in sheep's clothing, but inwardly they are ravening wolves."

I looked at her knowingly.

Then I glanced up front where Mama and Daddy were singing with the choir. I saw Daddy look at

Mama and smile.

I sighed and opened the worship service program.

A note was printed at the bottom of the page. "Today's flowers donated by Mr. and Mrs. Douglas Pierce."

Up front, the altar was adorned with two gorgeous vases filled with prize-winning Black-eyed Susans.

BETH SMITH is a wife, mother, grandmother, freelance writer, former, and retired public relations/communications director. As a freelance writer, her news and feature stories appeared in local publications, including the *Baltimore Sun, Baltimore Magazine*, and *Style Magazine*. "Love Among the Black-eyed Susans" is Beth's first foray into fiction.

Patti and The SUN

By Melisa Peterson Lewis

He wanted to know he could return to a predictable life, one with me waiting for him at home every day, dinner set, his slippers by the door. My husband John insisted on the purchase of our row home before he left for the war in Vietnam. He was not drafted like many men were. Instead he proudly enlisted. Even though he'd been away two years, he remained the Sun around which my world orbited. The key to our house reminded me of him and his plans for when he returned. He had placed the key in my hand and kissed me palm, promising me the world would be our oyster.

The small row home in Baltimore, Maryland was on a quiet street, filled with moms and children. Every weekend I would crouch down alongside my neighbors and scrub the marble stoops. The chitter chatter of woman was friendly and rhythmic. I enjoyed these weekends, and they helped me socialize and feel a sense of community that I desperately needed.

The airstrikes started, and more of our boys were dying. Mothers and wives fell silent when the mailman made his rounds. Russian roulette. Where will he stop? That day it was me. I felt the mailman hovering over me, his outstretched hand clenched a Western Union telegram from the Secretary of the Army. He said to me in a slow voice, "Oh, Patti. I'm sorry."

As a war widow, I was expected to act brave and march on, but I was also openly pitied. I was forced to ask for money from John's parents, and then my own. It was humiliating but necessary. Both helped me for several months, but it was clear, I needed a job. Poor John. I know he would have hated the idea of me working, and truth was I did not want to work. Even with a degree in English Composition from Goucher College, I had never practiced writing outside of school. College was a social class expectation in my family. My sisters and I weren't expected to do anything with our degrees.

John and I were introduced to each other by our parents during my senior year. He encouraged my writing as a hobby and found it endearing. My heart ached. It was never supposed to be like this. We were to be like every other occupant on the block. He would work, and I would stay home with the children; the children we never had a chance to have.

The mold in which I placed myself was broken. Unsure of my other options, I decided to pursue a career in writing. There was only one game in town worth going after, *The Baltimore Sun*. In recent years *The Sun* had expanded into several markets, including developing offices overseas in Rome and India. Working would force me to go against John's plan. With no more choices I became a traitor.

I felt the full weight of John's absence as I dressed for my first interview. Using my parents' money, I bought new stockings and a purse to match my white shoes. The style dress was shorter than I thought appropriate for a widow, but I was not taking chances. I didn't want to come across as an uptight prude. My bob was quaffed with enough Aqua-Net to withstand a hurricane. Out the door, I went.

The *Baltimore Sun*'s building at Calvert and Centre

Streets was enormous and busy. Like an ant at a picnic, I tried not to get squashed. Everyone buzzed with a purpose and had air about them that made my heart race. I was lost, stupid; I felt sick and turned to walk away when someone linked their arm around mine.

"Hi, friend. Where you headed?" A girl with long flowing locks of red and a short brown dress turned me back towards the entrance.

I stumbled, "…I have an interview with Mr. Nelson."

"Ah ha. Fresh meat," she laughed short but wide; I could see her molars. "I'm kidding. Well, kind of. Watch out for his...never mind. Hey look, I'm Susan. I'm a research assistant in the newsroom. That's where Mr. Nelson is too. I'll take ya there."

She whisked me away. I was on the Susan ride, linked at the elbow. I would have run off if not for her. Susan became my ally and the best friend I needed.

Mr. Nelson looked to be sixty years old, though I'm sure he was much younger. His office filled with cigarette smoke and smelled of brandy. His hoarse voice pounded on my shoulders while he ranted on about the problems with women and what the job would entail. It appeared that women came and left this position frequently. He explained this by mentioning that everyone he hires has a baby and leaves, though I'm not sure that was the full truth.

During the interview Mr. Nelson spat out one question after another, giving me only seconds to answer, he often spoke over my answers telling me "that's fine." I was hired on the spot and sent to work immediately as a print editor's assistant for a group of grumpy old men. The title was loose as I later found out. Often Susan and I would find ourselves doing everything from research, interviews, copy, editing, writing, and jumping as high as anyone told us to jump.

It was a hard job, but it was my job I had earned.

Mr. Nelson would call me into his office to blow off steam about something or another. Sales, lack of content, recants, and the war were all revolving fuses. His wife, Milly Nelson, was a significant topic of conversation. Three days into the job I was introduced to Milly. She wore a pink mink coat even in July. Her boobs were pushed up and separated so harshly I wondered if they had their own weather system. The heat would begin to peel away the layers of her make-up. When she blotted the white tissue came away beige. Susan and I called her Mrs. Hot Dog, and she treated us like her personal assistants. Mr. Nelson would chuckle when his wife acted as if she didn't realize how poorly she regarded us.

Soon after I started, I realized why so many girls left the job. It was a testosterone-driven climate, and at the head of it was Mr. Nelson. His hands would graze the nape of my neck while I was head down earnestly typing away. Often, he would ask questions about my living alone, offer me drinks any time I entered his office, and thank me for bringing heaven to work on days I wore a dress. I never let my guard down or shut the door to his office when I needed to speak to him.

In time, I began to love the newsroom despite my previous thoughts on owning a career and my boss. I swam in chaos with a pride. The flurry of men talking in ways I didn't hear men speak outside; women clicking away at their typewriters, phones ringing and being slammed down, shouting, laughing, the occasional crying. I loved the scene and being part of it. The smell of cigarettes burned the air mixing with the odors of salty paper and inky chemicals. When I worked late into the night, the smoke would clear, and I could feel the silence in my bones. It brought me closer to John. I would talk to him alone in the newsroom as I sat typing final copy or making edits. The tap of each letter echoed, and my fingers tap danced through the night. Leaving meant going back to my empty home. A cave with no light or warmth.

John. How I still missed him. The key to our home reminded me of his American dream. The key taunted me with the life I would never get to live. Even with his fashioned ways, John meant well. After almost a year of trying to hold myself up to John's plan, I began to realize the rest of my life couldn't be carved around his ghost. Coming to these terms made his death real all over again. I knew I had to let him go. I cried harder than when the telegram marking his grave was put in my hand. It was time for me to live without his presence, and it terrified me.

I was not alone; I had my family and Susan who was like a sister to me, even when she met a fellow who had proposed marriage. She insisted she would continue to work, and it surprised me when he allowed her to do so. I was happy for her but hated myself for the jealousy that beat in my chest. Alone, I was stained with the war widow title that so many of us carried. I wanted something else.

Thinking about next steps did not come naturally for me. Though with time it became clear I needed to ask for more pay and to have my name included under any of my work that was published. Several women wrote and co-wrote articles only to have their male counterparts receive the full credit in print. Most of the woman sat by and allowed this to happen, while others voiced their frustration. Those who got too vocal were often let go. I had to play this carefully. It took me days to practice my delivery for Mr. Nelson and to build the gumption I needed to face him.

Staring at myself in the mirror I practiced my speech, "Mr. Nelson. It is a pleasure to work here, and I have put in a lot of effort with the newsroom. I would like...NO. I need a raise to continue working here. Furthermore,

I want my name printed under the articles which I assist and write. It is only fair." My reflection bore back at me loud and confident. The Patti in the mirror made me proud, I wanted to be her all the time.

The next morning with my chin held high; I marched into Mr. Nelson's office prepared with my speech. Another news girl was sitting in front of his desk; tears streaked her face. My expression dropped as she rushed past me her burying her face in her hands. I looked at Mr. Nelson who acted as if someone told him today would be perfect golfing weather.

"Patti. What can I do ya for?" his grin stretched over his creased cheeks. He tapped a cigarette on the desk and then lit it. Nodding to offer me one; I shook my head.

"I've come to talk to you about my work."

"I see. Well, come on in!" He stood from his desk and escorted me into his office. Motioning with one hand for me to sit, he turned to close the door behind us. Lighting a cigarette, he took a seat on the front of his desk, in my direct line of vision was his tie weight.

Being shut off to the outside world with Mr. Nelson, I felt like a mouse in the snake's cage. I was betraying my senses as a woman and fear pelted my gut. I took a deep breath and belted into what I rehearsed.

"Mr. Nelson. I have been working here for some time, and I think a raise and credit where..."

"Patti. Patti," he threw his hands up in defense. Standing he walked over and put his hands on my shoulders. The cigarette in his hand came dangerously close to my hair, the smoke's warmth filled my ear. "Sweetheart look here. I like you. So, I'm going to see what I can do. Favor? Don't go mentioning this to those other girls, okay? I'm sure we can work something out quietly." His hand with the cigarette remained planted on my shoulder, while the other grazed down my sternum and around my waist towards my bottom. Before he could squeeze, I took a step back.

"Yes, sir. Thank you for your time." I forced a smile and left the room. My face burned, but I bit back tears.

At lunch, I unloaded on Susan. It all poured out—missing John, creating my dream, the men at the office stealing credit for our work, our creepy boss and his evil wife. She clasped my hand and said, "Patti, what is it that you really want here?"

"I want to be empowered! I want credit where it's due. I want a raise. I want my boss to keel over."

"Babe, let's try to narrow that list down. If you could have one thing, maybe not the one where you kill your boss, which would it be?" Her soft eyes told me not to give up.

"I want to be recognized for my work. My entire life I've lived on my parents or John's plan. I want something that's mine."

"If only there were a way to get your name in the paper without Mr. Nelson knowing it was you."

"Susan? I have a radical idea. What if I used my maiden name, Peterson, along with my shortened first name? My name would be Pat Peterson."

"That's not bad! When you write an article, sign that name. It's a man's name! No one will know, there are hundreds of writers here. Then one day when you're ready, WHAM! You confess, and the credit is all yours."

Clarity aroused the proud Patti I had seen in the mirror. I thought, maybe I can be that girl. I sat in silence considering this while Susan tried to read my face. "I'm going to do it."

The idea was far out, but the paper could print 60 pages some days and articles were jammed in tighter than sardines. I wanted to take a chance and hope no one would notice. Before I lost my courage, I decided to try it that very day. My male counterpart was assigned a story that he brushed off and passed on to me. It was a small article on Attman's Deli and their famous corned beef sandwiches. The line to get into Attman's was circling the block; Baltimore was head over heels. It was a small article but destined to be read.

I walked across the newsroom floor with the article neatly typed in my sweaty hand. The by-line read Pat Peterson. I dropped the piece in Mr. Nelson's inbox and stared. The metal bin seemed to sway, and the floor felt like it was tipping to the right. I nearly fainted. My nerves were doing me in. Susan cleared her throat from a few steps away, bringing me back to life. Walking away I felt as if everyone knew what I had done. I was a fraud, surely, I would be caught and hung.

That night the sheets on my bed tangled around my restless body. At 4 AM the phone startled me. Only having one phone, I ran downstairs to catch it.

"Patti! Did you see it?" It was Susan screaming into the receiver. "Pat Peterson is published! I couldn't help myself. I went to the loading dock to grab the first copy! It's you! You did it!"

"Unreal. That's just…unreal."

"You did it…" her voice followed the phone to the ground. With numb hands and a bottomed-out jaw, I shook my head. I was in print. Then I noticed the key to my row home lying on the table. Only for the first time, it represented my dream and not John's.

Melisa Peterson Lewis has self-published over 100 short stories and personal essays on her blog Fingers to Sky. Her first novel about an infection that overtakes Baltimore City is to be published by the end of 2019.

Tilly and the Sykesville Sasquatch

By Melisa Peterson Lewis

The trail grows dark, but Tilly continues towards the stream, confident she will turn up a crayfish or two for dinner. She wears most of the clothing she owns, including two scarves wrapped tightly around her hair and a pair of men's shoes she dug out of the trash. Waddling to the rocky streambed, she hums the song Zippity Doo Dah. Tilly is in her element. She and her husband, Ernie had lived off this land since the beginning. Her unmarked lot backs up to the Patuxent River and provides her with the essentials to exist. The silence of the woods is only interrupted by conversations she has with herself now that she is alone. She fiddles with the silver ring on her crooked pinky, the remaining memory of Ernie.

"Oh, look here. I bet there's a critter hiding under that rock!" With enthusiasm she jabs a golf club under the rock and flips it. The water turns murky, but her prize flicks its tail and shoots backwards. Tilly is fast, she scoops it up with a wire colander and drops it into a trash bag.

"Ha! Thought you were cleverer than me? Not today my friend, not today." She licks her lips and aims for another rock. After eleven crayfish tangles in the bottom of her bag, she heads towards home.

A flock of grackles screech and fly off. She curses at

the startle and places her hand on her drumming heart. Up ahead a sizeable dark animal darts between the trees.

"A bear?" The dark beast bends behind a thicket, making it hard to see. Tilly hears a grunt and tucks herself close to a broad oak, readying her golf club in case of an attack. Her hands are slippery with perspiration, and she silently counts her breaths to slow them.

A rustle in the leaves indicates the animal is close. Tilly's muscles tense. Using the element of surprise, she lunges out of hiding, swinging the golf club and screams, "Get out of here bear!"

Her club makes contact with a mound of fur; her elbows and teeth vibrate from the impact. She hears, "Oophf!" which is not the sound she expected. Tilly steps back to reevaluate the intruder. A man stands, shielding his head and stumbles backward tripping over a tree root. He calls out in pain as his elbow cracks on a rock.

The man barks, "Oey! Bloody hell! What ya do that for, ya old coot?"

"Excuse me?! You shouldn't sneak up on an old lady like that! You got what you deserve." Tilly realizes her belongings are strewn across the ground and begins to pick them up, never taking her eyes off the man on the ground.

He is wearing a fur cloak looking as if it were made from a dog. Most of his visible skin is covered in dark, coarse unkempt hair. A strap across his chest reveals a bag that clanks as if full of scrap metal. Tilly reaches up to her scarf and pats the greasy hair hiding beneath. She wonders, if he is like her?

"You there. Where do you come from?"

"Is it the accent that gives me away?"

"What are you doing here."

"Would you believe me if I said camping? Look, lass,

you really knocked me a good one. How about a hand, heh?"

Tilly observes the man, his elbow bleeds through a torn sweater, and he clutches his chest where she whacked him.

"I don't have much to help with," she said.

"Clean water?"

"Well, depends on your definition of clean."

Seemingly satisfied with this answer, he stands and walks towards her like a genetically altered bear. His long cloak drags behind his tall stiff stature.

"My definition of clean is flexible," he says.

Tilly nods and leads him away. Her home is crumbling. Green asphalt shingles fall from the walls and roof of her house, a tree grows through the front porch, and most of the windows are broken. Her yard is full of barrels, a fire pit made of stone and brick, and random treasures she cannot part with. He moves towards her house, but Tilly puts up her hand.

"Not there, I don't live in the house anymore. My treasures took over, and now I can't get them out or get me back in. Here." She points to an old van with tires held in place by wooden blocks. "It's small, but it does for me."

"Oh. I'm sorry dear," he responds.

"Sorry for what? This is my castle and I ain't never gonna leave. It's got everything I need and more."

"Right then."

The oddities Tilly calls "treasure" are only things she can appreciate; a keg tub as a seat, a piece of plywood held up by tires, and a canvas shopping bag that hangs high above her camp. She sees him eye the bag.

"It's so animals don't get my food."

"Right, makes sense."

He touches his elbow and grimaces. Tilly leans towards him and notices a musk she hadn't smelled before.

"How long you been out here?" She believes he is similar to her, which leaves her with questions. There might not be room for more than one woods dweller, so she is eager to know his story. "I tell ya what. I'm gonna cook up these crayfish and have some green beans. It's not much, but I'll share."

"Thank you—sorry, where are my manners. What is your name dear?"

"Matilda, though they call me Tilly." As she says this, she realizes no one has asked for her name in years. Her youngest daughter moved away when she was fifteen, and she hasn't seen her since. Even the soup kitchen at St. Joe's is visited in silence. She's grown used to being invisible.

"Pleased to meet you, Tilly, I'm Bernie. They call me the Sykesville Sasquatch."

"They do what?"

"It's a funny story really. I was fishing at my favorite watering hole. See I like to move around a lot, but there are a few spots I care for. This man is also fishing. I wave to him, but he looks at me in such disgust that I couldn't really help myself. I growled at him, and then I ran off."

Tilly slaps her knee and bends over, her laughter can be heard through the entire state of Maryland, birds flee from their roost and a deer, previously hidden, canters away.

"You growled at him?" Tears stream down her face leaving streaks of pink skin; a bad cough replaces her snorts of laughter.

"I'm not sure why that's so funny. He was an arrogant snot."

Tilly takes a few deep breaths and regains her composure. "Okay, sorry. I haven't had company in—well ever. I've never had company. And tonight, I get to dine with a Sasquatch?"

"The lout told the police a large beast tried to attack him. It was in the Carroll County Times. The writer poked fun saying, and I quote, 'Local fisherman discovers the missing link, a real Sasquatch in Carroll County!'"

"Oh dear. I'm sorry."

"It's forced me to come out this way more. The locals are all over the woods looking around. Say, can I stay here for just a little while? Lay low?"

Tilly considers this; he is a stranger and is in fact very strange.

"Are you like me?" She asks, uncertain if it's out of fear or the desire to connect with someone again. She fiddles with the silver band on her finger, which leaves a green mark when disturbed. She probes further, "Why do you live in the woods? Answer me honestly, I can tell if you're lying. I have always been able to recognize when my children were fibbing." This she knows is right. Every promise her children made to visit or bring her warmer clothes were left unfulfilled. She saw annoyance in their faces the last time they came, which was two years ago.

His hesitation makes her wary.

"Okay lass. I'm going to tell you the full truth. I haven't told anyone this before, but what do I have to lose? I can always go back the way I came. Even though you owe me for hitting me like you did!"

"Humpf! You attacked me! I was defending myself." She bats the air and sours her expression.

"You want the story or not?"

"No need to shout. Go on."

"I'm from England. Been here for 7 years, living around Maryland and Pennsylvania. That fisherman wasn't the first to have spotted me, so I keep on the go."

"Why did you leave England?"

"It's not a good story Tilly. You sure you want to know?"

"I'm not letting a complete stranger stay here. Tell me." She knew this was unfair; she would never give up her own stories. Some were dark and buried, and it was her preference to keep them locked away.

"Okay then. I stole something from a significant person. The only way I could avoid being caught and murdered for my wrongdoing was to move far away. Even if I returned it today, I would be killed."

"Oh, dear god, what is it you stole?"

Bernie takes a seat on the keg tub, bowing his head to avoid Tilly's eye contact. "I was a grave digger. Some of the boys and I would steal jewelry and such before we put someone in the ground. I know it's horrible, but it helped us make ends meet, and the money became hard to pass up. This particular woman, I stole her wedding band, it was quite elaborate. When I went to pawn it, the man behind the counter recognized it as his deceased wife's ring. He pulled a shotgun out from behind the desk and fired it. Close range! He missed. I ran. When I got home, my mum told me to keep running. Everyone knew what I had done. I didn't look back. That was years ago." Bernie pats his chest, a thick cord around his neck indicates something hiding beneath his shirt.

Tilly holds her breath, her hands clench so tightly her dirty fingernails pierce her skin. This was a crime she hadn't expected. Instantly her gut tells her to turn him away, to run, hide, protect her belongings! Her treasures in her house suddenly feel exposed. Cursing herself, she maneuvers her hands behind her back to peel her own wedding ring from her knotty pinky finger and slip it into her pocket. Her last true treasure, the ring Ernie gave her when she told him he was going to be a dad.

"Tilly. I was a different man then. I would never do it

again. The earth has provided for me, it's all I need. Believe me." Bernie uses the back of his hand to rub his eye.

"That's horrible. Stealing from the dead? Your soul will have no rest for what you've done."

"Don't say that!"

"Send it back. Send it now. You don't even live in the country. They could never find you."

"It's all I have left of my homeland now. I can't part with it." Bernie openly weeps, his hands cover his face, and he sits back on the keg tub. A ring symbolizing a previously-lived life is something Tilly understands.

"You have sinned Bernie. A great horrible sin. Come to church with me tomorrow. They feed us, and you can talk to the pastor. He will know if God can forgive you." Tilly stretches her back to feel taller. In the face of adversity, she always turns to church. Pastor Robbins is a good man; she is sure he will know what to do.

Bernie snorts back his sob. "I can't go into town. There was a sketch with the article. Someone will recognize me as the Sykesville Sasquatch. Honestly, I've become warm to the name, but I don't want to have to explain myself to people." He smiles with his newfound celebrity status.

"Feeling a little famous?" Tilly laughs through her teeth at her joke.

"I tell ya what, you go to church and bring back new clothes and maybe some scissors to cut my hair. Then I'll go with you next time, a little more cleaned up."

Pondering this idea, Tilly realizes he will need to stay with her for a week. The idea is unsettling, but she agrees. Pastor Robbins would urge her to help the less fortunate just as the church has helped her. It's rather different being the person to lend a hand. Pride prickles through her skin, leaving goose bumps and raising arm hair.

"Okay. I agree."

The two hobos cook up crawfish and eat green beans straight from the can. Bernie sits atop the keg tub, and Tilly drags over a bucket which she flips and sits on. The two share stories about people who used to be in their lives and how quickly they disappear. The loneliness of the woods embraces them, yet it is also a one-way trap. Tilly explains when she started this life people wanted to help and change her, fix her. She never saw anything wrong with collecting treasures that made her feel safe and rich. Eventually those who seemed so concerned began to disappear, until no one, including her children, would come to visit.

Tilly was sure she was the only one living this way. How fortunate to have met a like-minded woodsman. Her eyes became warm and wet, knowing this encounter would end. She knew sadness would hover for years, joining the loss of others she mourned.

Night covers and cools the woods. Tilly makes up a bed of old clothing on the porch for Bernie. Good nights are exchanged, and she goes to the van. She wants to trust Bernie, but a woman can never be too sure about a man, so she locks the doors and drifts off to sleep.

The next morning Tilly wakes with the usual stiff knuckles and cold nose. Sitting up she stretches her arms up high. Letting out a big yawn she gasps at the green film around her pinky finger. Her ring is absent. She pats down the bed around her. Then she remembers, she had removed it after hearing Bernie's story. She tries to remember where she put it. Her hands run down her pants and into her pockets, then into her sweater. She was sure she put it in her sweater pocket. She checks her socks, then under her hair scarf, and in her shoes. It is nowhere. Her eyes start to dart and panic shocks her extremities.

She throws open the van door, which to her surprise was unlocked.

"Bernie!" She shouts, running towards the porch.

His bed lays untouched. Tilly crumbles to her knees, shaking her head and pumping a fist into the air, "No. No. No. I'm so stupid." She allows herself a deep cry, mourning her dead husband, and the loss of his ring.

"Tilly! You will not let him get away with this. NO!" She scolds herself for misjudging Bernie. Thief!

The sound of a van pulling up to the end of her long driveway halts her emotions. Time for church. She convinces herself Pastor Robbins will know what to do. A glimmer of hope stops her tears, and she hurries to the van with her usual trash bag in hand.

As soon as Tilly arrives at church, she launches into dialogue with anyone in earshot. At the end of the hour, she corners Pastor Robbins and relays her entire situation. Several others stand by. Their faces show concern and fear.

The church secretary leans in towards Tilly, "I'm sorry honey, but you're trying to tell us that a Sasquatch stole your wedding ring? Do you hear anything strange about your story?"

"He wasn't really a Sasquatch, he only growled because he was frustrated. He's English!"

The audience disperses, and she hears someone murmur, "Poor old thing. It might be time to call Protective Services."

Betrayal rolls over Tilly. This life she took so long to craft is spoiling. No one visits her; no one cares; no one listens. What is the point? She walks outside to the awaiting van to take her home.

Her pinky finger is naked, exposing her to the elements more than ever.

"Oh, Bernie. Why did you do it? I thought –"

"You say something, miss?" The driver asks.

"No, sorry."

She thinks of Bernie and the starry night they had together. Sucking the heads of the crayfish and eating vegetables out of a can. He made her laugh. She can't remember the last time anyone made her appreciate an emotion or pulled a feeling out of her crusty existence. Until last night she was passenger, going through the motions to stay alive. She fought for this charade to prove her children wrong. They had abandoned her, and as long as she was alive, she knew it hurt them to think of her.

Tilly understood that Bernie was like her. He knows solitude comes at a price. The price was a cheap silver ring worth nothing more than a memory. Bernie's sin wasn't stealing from the dead, it was stealing from the living. He stole that man's wedding gift to his wife, and now he stole a part of Tilly's soul leaving an empty space.

One thing Tilly is good at is filling voids with treasure. This has been her job since her husband had passed away. Tilly ponders the possibility of what would fill the vacant area Bernie has left behind. For the first time, she realizes a material thing will not suffice. The foreign thought invades her, if not material then what could it be?

Seven Postcards From My Unmarried Aunt Betsy Plus One Letter.

By Ellen Krawczak

Post Card 1 – June 1, 1955

Dear Alfred and Mindy, I was surprised when you told me that your entire neighborhood goes to Chesapeake Beach every Sunday at dawn during the summer. I'm not sure that I would want to get up at 6:00 am to spend time with people I can see every day. I know that your Ellen loves the water, but I can't help but be a bit worried. She is so fair haired and freckly. Aren't you afraid that she is getting too much sun? We would not want her skin to dry out. Wouldn't she be better off if she went to museums instead? The ones here in Spain are wonderful. Love, Aunt Betsy.

Post Card 2 – May 3, 1965

Dear Alfred, did you and Mindy really buy a sailboat? I guess that Ellen is growing up because you wrote that she crews for you when you race. Ellen is so shy; I'm not sure that spending summer weekends on a boat racing around Chesapeake Bay will help her socially. What do you think about enrolling her in finishing school over the summer? I would be happy to help pay. Love, Aunt Betsy. PS: Tel Aviv is busy and bustling – a marvelous city.

Post Card 3 – September 2, 1975

Dear Ellen, I am now living in Hong Kong. How grand that you are working and living in Baltimore. The Inner Harbor has terrific shopping and there are so many good restaurants in the city. You wrote that you love living near the water and taking long walks along the Inner Harbor promenade. I'm sure that is lovely, but it's probably not the best way to meet eligible young men. Have you thought about joining some type of social club? I'm sending you a silk scarf. Love, Aunt Betsy.

Post Card 4 – October 4, 1982

Dear Ellen, I saw the article in the newspaper about you and your friends learning to water ski on Deep Creek Lake. I'm sure that you are having fun, but honestly, water skiing is not in the same league as other socially acceptable sports. You are in your early thirties and it's time to think about your future. Tennis and golf clubs are such wonderful places to meet our type of people. I'm sending you a new tennis racket. Next stop on the tour is Thailand. Love, Aunt Betsy.

Post Card 5 – April 6, 1986

Dear Ellen. I'm loving Tahiti. Your parents wrote me that you moved to Harve de Grace, near the Susquehanna River, with your new husband. I hope that you are living inland. The Susquehanna River rises significantly and floods easily. It is not safe to be near such a major waterway. And, I hope you are not thinking about buying a boat again. That little boat that you had on the Nanticoke River was dangerous. You are too old to be risking your life, especially if you are planning to have children. I mean that in the kindest way. Love, Aunt Betsy.

Post Card 6 – July 20, 1995

Dear Ellen. It was so nice talking to you and catching up. You seem excited about your family vacation trip to Ocean City. Frankly, spending your days at the beach building sand castles sounds rather boring. Wouldn't the children prefer to be at math camp or dance camp learning something useful. (I'll pay). Who wants to come home and get into bed with sand between their toes? I hope you stay closer to home next year. New York has so much to offer. I still have a pied-a-terre in the city. Perhaps we can do lunch when you get home. Love, Aunt Betsy.

Post Card 7 – July 7, 2010

Dear Ellen, I've finally settled into my gorgeous independent living apartment in Hilton Head. This place has just the right kind of people. I heard that you bought a home on the St. Martin River in Ocean Pines. Well, I can't say that I'm too surprised. Did you ever stop to think that rivers rise, that they flood, that they become polluted, etc. I hope that you are drinking bottled water. Please be careful. The waterways are filled with weekend boaters who don't know what they are doing. Give your children and grandchildren a hug from me. Love, Aunt Betsy.

Letter 1- August 12, 2012

Dear Mrs. Ellen Kaye. We are so sorry to inform you that your Aunt Betsy passed away yesterday. She was lounging at the pool when a gust of wind picked up her lounge chair and tossed her into the water. She did not know how to swim and unfortunately drowned. Our lifeguard and medical team did their best to try to revive her. Please know that the staff here at Hilton Head Assisted Living did all they could. We will miss her.

We are so sorry for your loss. Please arrange for someone to clean out her room by the end of the month.
Sincerely,
The HHAL staff

ELLEN KRAWCZAK lives in the Ocean Pines Community on the lower eastern shore. She loves being on the St. Martin river, watching the ducks and listening to the birds.

Baltimore: Life on the Streets

By Suzanne McCoskey

As the car cruised down Light Street, I inhaled deeply. I love this city. It has its cuts and scars, that I know, but there is no place I would rather live. This city has made me who I am. I looked over at my partner. We have been together now for almost five years and we can communicate without speaking. He looked back at me and then turned his head away.

We turned onto Fort Avenue and I was struck again by the sense of familiarity in the row homes we passed. Some still maintained their formstone facades and some had been stripped down to their original red brick. It is a visual that, more than anything, tells me I am home. This city and its unapologetic expression of the cacophony of life … we get along this city and I … we understand each other.

We pulled up in front of a small brick rowhouse. The door was ominously open. "Here we go," I thought, "back on duty." The three-day break for Thanksgiving had come abruptly to an end.

The homeowner came over to us and took us inside the house. She looked distraught. Usually I let my partner handle this kind of situation—he is much better with people. I have been told I am a bit stubborn and intense.

We entered the home and the owner closed the door behind us. Her cell phone rang, and I heard her say, "I can't talk now, Mom, the house has been broken into ... I don't know, I just got home ... no, I am okay, but I'll have to call you back later." She walked through the main room and into the kitchen and I heard her make another call.

My partner and I started walking around the house, looking around for evidence from the theft. Didn't seem like there would be a lot to take, if I am being honest. It looked like the typical home of a young single woman just starting out on her own. The furniture was kind of grubby ... the tv small and outdated, left behind ... no real sign of expensive audio equipment, just an old clock radio on a side table. The owner ran over and looked at the open cabinet under the tv. "All my DVDs," she wailed. Well, so far nothing big. My partner had gone to check upstairs and the owner looked at me and then ran upstairs. "They got Grandma's watch," I heard her scream. I could hear the rising anxiety in her voice.

There was a knock on the door and the owner ran back downstairs and opened the door. A uniform cop entered, "Ma'am." She started talking rapidly and seemed on the edge of hysteria. I saw my partner on the steps and walked over to join him. Better to let her focus on telling her story once and get it all out. She looked like she was about to lose it. I heard her take a breath and say:

"Officer, do you watch Homicide: Life on the Street?" Oh, no, I thought, here we go ...

The homeowner pointed to me and my partner sitting on the stairs watching them. Well, I guess I could call her our owner, not just the homeowner, but I hate that expression. "Those guys' names are Bayliss and Pembleton."

I couldn't read his expression. Couldn't tell if he was a cat person or not. "Bayliss and Pembleton, huh. Where were you two guys when they rolled this joint?"

I saw the smile break out on our owner's face. I was

afraid she was going to start crying and now she was laughing. This guy's good, I thought. I love this city.

SUZANNE MCCOSKEY uses her training in statistics and economics to pay her bills but her love for the city of Baltimore feeds her soul.

Essays

Sailing the Chesapeake
By Daniel Rosenblum

When the sky turns an irresistible azure and the wind snaps at my cheek, I yearn for the broad Chesapeake Bay, full of surprises. Although the Bay offers many options, it's sailing on her that pulls me in. The wind's unsure, but if my wife and I catch it right, the day might supply an antidote to the headaches at home.

Whatever the risks, a nippy wind and glorious sky will find us heading for the marina early in the day. We'll grab chips and sandwiches, fill the jug, and sling some towels and swim suits in a tote. Slathered in suntan lotion and decked out in dark glasses and rubber-soled shoes, we'll head off on the John Hanson Highway for Annapolis. Berthed on the Back Creek and at the ready, our sailing sloop, the Zephyr, awaits her energetic crew.

We'll have company in the mouth of the Severn. On a fine day, passionate sailors push to reach the Bay early when the wind is up. Let's hope they're sober, for the chances of a collision will multiply if they're not. We might catch a view of migratory birds, an osprey or two, or even a large sailboat crewed by a classful of midshipmen from the Naval Academy.

God help the skippers who ignore the channel markers. "Red right return!" I want to yell at them, but I hold my peace. With luck, a flood tide will forgive them their errors and spare them from getting mired in the mud.

We'll gladly give way to the kayaks and sailing dinghies, even when they tack across our bow unexpectedly. We'll be out on the Bay in a quarter of an hour. Inspired by the promise of freedom, we'll take our time in the channel, while we enjoy the verdant landscape, the thick clusters of trees basking in the sun, and the regal homes serene on their plush lawns, high above the water.

When no one's in our way, our sails will fill, carrying us to the open water at five or six knots. My wife will take the tiller while I hoist the main, then I'll replace her at the helm. As the breeze picks up, we'll ready the jib.

Entering the open Bay, I'll turn upwind. I'll watch as my wife lets the breeze blow fan her hair, sharing her excitement. She'll laugh as it tickles her skin. I'll laugh, too, as my cares drift behind me in the sailboat's wake.

We'll have a choice of destinations, but one of our favorites is to head for the Bay Bridge. Off we'll go, tacking upwind, as soon as we catch sight of the graceful spans arching high above the water. With luck, we'll pass under the bridge in an hour or two, leaving time for lunch and a good run on the homeward leg.

Out on the Bay we can see forever or, if not, it seems like it. Huge cargo ships from Asia move swiftly toward Baltimore, bearing rafts of containers, piled so high you'd think they might topple over on a high sea. Better keep well away from their sterns, for their turbulent wake can entrap a sailboat. Same goes for tugboats pulling barges. Their steel tow-lines can be both treacherous and invisible. Kite boarders surfing, when the water's just right, and trimarans, even when it isn't, go scooting across the water faster than the wind, defying common sense.

On other days, if time permits, we'll overnight in one of the charming villages on the Eastern Shore, like Oxford or St. Michael's. More distant islands have their appeal, although mariners may be greeted with shotguns, if they don't obtain permission in advance.

If the wind changes, our fondest dreams may end in despair. A westerly can bring in a front, causing a bright day to end in a miserable squall and stirring up choppy waves that make for a bumpy ride. Bright beginnings don't always make for happy endings.

Whatever the wind, I love the journey, but with no wind at all even a faithful Bay-lover may develop a roving eye. Whenever I'm caught in the doldrums, I chase the devil in me with my tongue. I rekindle my romantic fire with inventive stories, as much to lift the sagging interest of my invited guests as my own. If I can get them to laugh at my foolishness, I can yet save the day.

I find myself spinning yarns about my misadventures, reminding them that the Bay's part river, part ocean. Her briny currents come from the sea, I tell them. The Susquehanna and other rivers bring her tons of mud. Ribbons of shallow shoals permeate her nether parts, like wings they festoon her depths miles from her shore. Novices who venture out armed with road maps and six packs are vulnerable to her snares.

I'll recall how, years ago, in love with sailing smaller boats, but knowing nothing about the larger ones, I rented a sloop with a deep keel, invisible from above the water but big enough to reach a bottom less than four feet from the surface. A sudden bump preceded a dawning awareness of a lack of any other boats in the part of the Bay where I was sailing. The absence of other craft was a sign I would later come to respect. I was mired on a shoal. I richly deserved the withering expression on the Coastie's face. Wordlessly, I felt his eyes telling me that lightbulbs of my low wattage were best kept off the water. Towing us off the shoals could get old. He pointed to the Thomas Point Light.

"It's more than two miles away," I said, feebly.

"All the worse," he said. "You should be on the far side of it. Next time use a nautical chart instead of a road map. You're lucky you didn't tear a hole in the hull."

Turned out, the man who towed us was remarkably friendly and happy to give us suggestions to keep ourselves out of danger. My relationship with the Chesapeake blossomed under the guidance of the Coast Guard, veteran sailors, and others already gripped by her charms. They helped me develop the savoir faire for keeping these waters untroubled; they showed me how to navigate, give way, signal, pass harbor markers, and handle breakdowns and emergencies. They taught me what I needed to know before I skippered a boat on the Chesapeake, the importance of learning their measurements, designs, capacities, and mechanics. I learned to tie a bowline and other sailor's knots without thinking twice about them. I picked up skills that helped me read the clouds and smell approaching squalls. Competent captains coached me in the elegant manners of the best skippers, the ones who display self-discipline and coolness, understatement and receptiveness. From them I learned that guests and crew take their cues from the captain; a cool skipper keeps everyone calm.

After regaling my guests with a bit of sailor talk, we'll break out the guacamole and chips, and chatter on, waiting for the wind to pick up, motoring back to the slip as a last resort.

Even if the weather proves fickle, the Bay remains a steady presence in my life. She always welcomes me. Even on a foggy day she has possibilities.

Rain or shine, we enjoy the adventure. Give us a cloudless sky or the barest glimmer of sunlight, a gusty wind or an almost breathless zephyr. We'll take it.

Dan Rosenblum is a retired physician and former sailor on the Chesapeake, who is writing a memoir about his family and himself. He became a war orphan after his father, also a physician, was lost at sea during WWII while serving on a Coast Guard weather ship in the North Atlantic.

A Foot in Both Worlds
By T. J. Butler

I'm a recent transplant from the city to semi-rural life on Maryland's Chesapeake Bay. For just a few seasons, I've lived in a place where the stars are visible every night, where the months of the year are discernible by the abundant foliage and what the waterman are selling, and by the prevalence of roadkill. My previous experience with roadkill was limited to squirrels fallen from power lines while attempting to cross the street, and I regularly drove on avenues named after positions in a royal court. Today, my daily byways and country roads have names like Swamp Circle and Muddy Creek Road, and I would like to believe the colorfully named Buck Fever Way is posted at the beginning of a long private driveway, rather than a public road.

In my new and less populated region, I occasionally feel like an onlooker with a foot in both worlds. Daily, I observe and absorb the details of a culture markedly different than what I'm familiar with. I've gleaned that there is neither a right or a wrong way of doing things, only different ways for different people. I have taken strides, albeit small ones, to assimilate myself since I have chosen to call the bay my home, however, there is still a wide gulf between my city self and a future self who might be mistaken for one of the locals.

Living on the bay, I'm regularly struck by the fact that my formerly urgent and spirited nautilus of metropolitan concerns was very small. In my new home, surrounded by unfamiliar local customs, I've found that the places where strangers say hello, where the roads are long and straight, and where the heavens are visible at night make up a great big world that is far, far larger than me.

My primary motivation for relocating to the water is namely the draw of coastal living and the opportunities for sailing; however, the expansive darkness of the night sky, and a nearby acreage perpetually housing baby goats and miniature horses have indeed sweetened the deal. In addition to the prevalence of knee-high animals near my home, we have produce stands and frequent deer sightings at dusk. I especially enjoy driving by fields of crops or horses bordered by wooden fences and the requisite barns, both abandoned and in use, and the equivalent number of vacant houses crumbling into scenes of picturesque overgrowth. Previously, all these things involved a road trip, and while they are now close to home, the novelty of seeing deer and viewing the stars at night has not worn off.

Although my new home is less populated than the city, it is not the backwoods of provincial stereotypes, being an hour as the crow flies from the large and thriving metropolis that makes the wheels of the world spin. Additionally, in thirty traffic-free minutes, I can be in the flourishing state capital with its town centers and chain restaurants.

Closer to home, our principal thoroughfares are two-lane roads dotted in the middle to allow for the passing of slow-moving farm machinery. Scores of formerly urban dwellers reside just off these country roads while maintaining jobs in the city and I count myself among these transplant commuters. We travel daily to the glass, concrete, and steel metropolis, and many of us have similarly fled the city to escape the urban sprawl, to consume seafood as fresh as the breeze blowing off the bay, and to live every day like a coastal vacation.

Spring Chicken Supper

Along the scenic roads near my new home, fire departments and civic organizations frequently post signs advertising group meals, creating a bounty of foodstuffs set forth in town halls and church basements. As winter gives way to spring, the Fraternal Order of the Local Farmer hosts their annual Spring Chicken Supper. This is not a clever play on words. It is, in fact, a chicken dinner held in the spring. I'm unaware of whether the double entendre was intentional or lost on the association's social director. Churches and other associations often sponsor pancake dinners in which families of all stripes can dine on traditional breakfast fare at night, and the vast numbers of organizations that sponsor spaghetti dinners make one ponder the hidden significance of pasta and meat sauce.

In urban areas, the best patches of grass for signage are on curbs and concrete islands at busy intersections. The most common signs confidently promise to help you earn fast cash with no selling, or offer to buy any junk car for $200, call now. There is nary a Spring Chicken Supper sign for many miles. Alternately, the ubiquitous signs at every crossroads near my home on the bay are friendly, welcoming, and you can always find a good meal if you look closely.

While I've never attended a pancake social or spaghetti dinner, I have an idealized vision of the first time I'll get a craving for breakfast-for-dinner on the very day of the pancake fest.

Me: Have you seen those pancake dinner signs?
Husband: No.
Me: Are you hungry?

Husband: No.

Me: I have a twenty dollar bill. Let's go get pancakes.

Husband: Can we bring the dog?

My husband and I will pile into his Jeep, sans dog, and drive the long way to the main road, passing numerous crossroads because I won't remember where I saw the sign. We'll pass signs advertising fresh cut hay, deer corn, school bus drivers wanted, and fill dirt for sale, and we'll eventually locate the sign. We'll then arrive at a nondescript VFW hall or Elk's Lodge bordered by native flowers in mulch beds. Jeeps, pickups, and minivans will be parked in the grass, as the early birds will have already filled the lot.

I imagine that for the price of admission, ten dollars apiece at the door, we'll be greeted with a smile so genuine I'll assume my husband has been previously acquainted with the smiler. While we're in line for our pancakes, hash browns, and a choice of link or patty sausage, I envision a woman standing next to us will strike up a conversation. We'll chat about the weather, the local sheriff's election, and which of the volunteers has the best garden this season. "I saw Cynthia's beans, and they were so much larger than mine. I bet she's fertilizing with eggshells. My Bob drinks so much coffee that I've got the grounds coming out my ears, and grounds fertilize best in the garden for greens." She'll then lower her voice in a slightly conspiratorial tone and continue. "I'm not telling tales out of school, mind you, but you can do so much more with greens on the supper table."

I'll initially be taken aback by the genuine camaraderie, and my knee-jerk response may be "Hmm, so what do you do," because this rote statement has been ingrained into my adult meeting-new-people repertoire.

If this practiced but meaningless remnant from the city makes it past my lips, I'll be met with hobbies, family obligations, and anything but work. I'll be struck once again that there are those who live to work and others who work to live, and it is not hard to speculate on which set also enjoys pancakes.

    Our plates will be mounded over with the fluffiest pancakes of all, and my husband and I will search the room for two seats together as we slowly carry our plates through the hall. Initially, we'll find no seats available as we pass the rows of long, scuffed cafeteria tables and tan metal folding chairs. However, we'll begin to notice kindly diners making room for us as we pass. Once we find seats, we'll be welcomed with smiles from around the table. There will be genuine greetings through mouthfuls of home fries, and nods and introductions between sips of rich steaming Folger's Crystals.

    Nary a dining companion will inquire about our jobs. Instead, they'll want to discuss our dog, whether the fish are biting, and this early in the season, can you believe how the weather's been? As we finish our plates in the bosom of our new flapjack fellowship, I'll imagine that we've been accepted and received without pause and we'll gladly accept an invitation to the upcoming Chops & Potatoes Luncheon.

In the city we've left, the roadside signage generally promises fantastic opportunities for untold wealth with no selling in only a few short days. These incredible claims do not come with pancakes, but if they did, we would surely not be invited. One must pause to consider that there are areas today where a sign for pancakes can bring hungry citizens together as a community, and other areas where the signs boast of empty promises, and breakfast for dinner rarely includes your neighbors.

The Turkey Shoot

Last fall brought a large sign to the busiest local crossroads advertising a seasonal event, a turkey shoot, with another form of meat prominently listed as the featured menu item. It bears repeating that despite my pancake family fantasy, I'm not yet well versed in the cultural minutiae found beyond that of my former city limits. Culture aside, I was taken aback the first time I saw the colorful, festive sign depicting an exaggeratedly smiling cartoon turkey and the urgent, excited red bubble lettering spelling out, "Turkey Shoot."

I drove home imagining a sad and crushingly similar interpretation of shooting fish in a barrel in which dozens of turkeys were put into a field. For the price of admission, I envisioned these birds made into living targets for those who fancied themselves cunning hunters yet wanted no part in spending the day in a hunting blind covered in deer urine. Please be reminded that I am still making efforts to assimilate myself into Chesapeake Bay culture; the fact that I not only took special notice of the Turkey Shoot sign but became incensed by it does nothing more than to peg me as an outsider who drives around mesmerized by common roadside signs.

Although I am open to learning about local ways, I could not help feeling this event was somehow wrong. In my growing disdain of the turkey shoot, I imagined not wild turkeys capable of minimal flight, but rather, fat, round butter balls with giant breasts. These rotund and juicy beasts surely would not have the strength to heft their girth from the ground. I followed this contemptuous train of thought by imagining these very turkeys with clipped wings, further adding insult to the inevitable injury sure to follow in the upcoming affair. Due to the ubiquitous local hunting culture, this distasteful form of shooting turkeys in a barrel was something I reluctantly yet tacitly agreed to disagree with the local populace about. I could not, however, resign myself to accept the most unforgivable detail; turkey was not even featured on the menu.

As I'm wont to do when faced with unfamiliar concepts, I queried the internet for the most likely yes or no answer: "Do they shoot turkeys at a turkey shoot?" With relief, I learned that a turkey shoot involves shooting at paper targets with frozen turkeys bestowed upon the winners. Now, this was something I could really get behind! Shooting paper targets for sport occurs daily at gun ranges, yet frozen turkeys are rarely awarded as prizes. Here at my very own crossroads, between the sign showing in removable numbers the county's annual opioid death and overdose count, and the adjacent sign advertising the preparation of freshly killed deer into jerky, sausage, and steaks, was an event featuring the centerpiece of a traditional holiday meal as the coveted prize. I carried on smugly, knowing that my new and resounding approval of the turkey shoot would put me one step closer to understanding the culture of the bay.

The Onion Van

Last spring I stopped at a thriving, expansive farm stand, the type one would expect to offer not only a variety of fruits and vegetables but also a wide selection of ancillary homemade favorites. There is no comparison to the convenience of one-stop shopping for a bounty of colorful pick't-fresh produce, baked goods, and jars of local honey, dilly beans, and chow chow, all laid out on broad, sun-warmed, chipped wooden tables.

I stopped at this farm stand not because my pantry was bare but because I was running an errand nearby and had few remaining commitments that afternoon. Additionally, a pint of local berries would make me feel less like I was wasting the farm-to-table culture than if I'd purchased them from the grocery store. Unfortunately, the chipped wooden tables were sparsely laden with hothouse cucumbers and tomatoes, and a host of late-season winter greens and root vegetables. The seller gloomily informed me that the growing season had begun late due to winter's multiple and insistent encores of unseasonably frigid weather.

With little to do but chat with the seller, I immediately mentioned living nearby and driving into town for my errand. I wanted to appear as someone other than an outsider who drove a long way to procure produce from the country. I bent to snuggle the small dog that bounded up to me, barked a tiny bark, and immediately licked my hand. "Oh," I crooned as I scratched behind its ears. "You're such a little puppersnapper!" The seller leaned against the counter and proudly told me a heartwarming tale of adopting the dog from the local high-kill shelter. This led to a discussion about her husband, and we moved casually into her divulging salacious details about the nearby Amish farm's winter tomato growing technique.

"The secret is to plant them in the ground, but you've also got to keep them warm," the seller stated knowingly. I learned that only tomatoes planted in the ground are imbued with a real, honest-to-God homegrown taste, not like in the contemptuous raised plywood beds of her farm stand competitors. Oh no, these Amish knew their soil. "And you know how they do it?" she leaned in, lowered her voice, and in a tone akin to revealing dark secrets of the vegetable variety, pronounced that the Amish keep not one, but two wood stoves burning in their sturdy greenhouses all winter. "Not one, but two," she repeated to emphasize the ingeniousness of the Amish. "You've got to keep the place warm and what with only one stove, with our winters here what would happen to the plants if it went out?"

Thus, the conversation segued to The Onion Van. I described a recent weekend drive into town when I'd driven past a series of roadside signs hawking onions. Onions and onions alone were advertised on each sign, and I quickly visualized the most delicious caramelized onion tart there ever was. This imaginary tart grew more scrumptious with each sign, and I resolved to stop at nothing to attain a large bag of farm-fresh onions from this single-vegetable vendor. Unfortunately, the tart of my dreams was dashed to pieces in the roadside gravel as I approached and subsequently sped past the seller who loomed menacingly on the side of the road.

The farm stand, if I may be so bold as to call it that, was nothing short of an unmarked forest green van, and to stress it's threatening appearance, let me state that it had no windows. Little girls the world over are taught to recognize that "stranger danger" comes in many forms, and I can smell a dangerous van from a mile away. A crudely lettered wooden sign leaned against the van with a single scrawled word, onions, and it was not even capitalized. The Onion Van was parked adjacent to a road leading deep into the forest, quite possibly the very primrose path that carries people to places miles from where anyone can hear them scream. I am worldly enough to know that caramelized onion tarts, no matter how deeply sweet and flavorful, are not worth a treacherous stop at The Onion Van.

I relayed my brush with imminent danger to the farm stand proprietress with enough melodrama and showmanship that I was sure she'd ask for my recipe and congratulate me for safely buying onions at the grocery store. Instead, I was vexed and humiliated when she recognized the van's forest green color and morosely replied, "That was Mr. Wilkins. His wife died two months ago, and he's been lost without her." As I gracelessly and abruptly left the farm stand empty-handed and flushed with embarrassment, I realized I was not the type of person worthy of knowing secrets about Amish tomatoes and wood stoves.

I have been around the block a few times, and rarely do I get the opportunity to say, "Why yes, this is my first rodeo." I am aware of my surroundings and rarely walk alone in dark alleyways; I am a woman in early middle age with no children, so I'm usually safely home drinking wine after dark. I am savvy enough to differentiate between the dangers found in fear-mongering forwarded emails and the legitimate perils that come from strangers, not going to the gym enough, and getting too close to unmarked vans. Unfortunately, the farm stand experience taught me two things; my innate, fundamental, and misguided cautions caused me to miss out on a heavenly bag of Chesapeake Bay onions. Additionally, I missed the opportunity to pointedly tell a local farmer that I, too, live nearby, as if to prove that I am not the outsider I actually still am. Primarily, though, the experience has conspicuously brought to light that my underlying suspicions are no longer the one size fits all mindset of my former city existence.

I have learned two additional lessons from the onion van; there is such a thing as gossiping at the farm stand, and no good can ever come of it. With the onion van's owner humanized, it is apparent that instead of being spirited away in a cleverly disguised van with no windows, I missed out on a genuine human connection. Also, possibly, I missed out on a conversation about just what it is that makes an onion tick. Coffee grounds as fertilizer? Amish wood stoves? Good old bay air?

I now make strides to gossip about harmless local

topics such as blue crabs, homegrown tomatoes, deer jerky, and miniature horses. I silently cheer for the grand prize winner of every turkey shoot in the region. I try to blend in, and one day soon, I hope it will come naturally. Additionally, I'd like to be less an observer of this new, foreign culture and become more of a participant because now, the bay is my home. In keeping with these efforts and desires, I can assure you that my latest caramelized onion tart, baked with only the finest local farm stand onions, was richer and more exquisite than I could have ever imagined.

T. J. Butler lives on a sailboat with her husband and dog. She writes short fiction that is not all fun and games. She is a Pushcart Prize nominee and a contributor to *Tiny House Magazine*. Her work appears or is forthcoming in *Barren, Flash Fiction Magazine, Anti-Heroine Chic, Quail Bell, Soft Cartel,* and others.

The Bridge

By Donna Rothert

The Chesapeake Bay Bridge, opened in 1952 and expanded in 1973, is 4.3 miles of steel and concrete joining two geographical halves of Maryland in more ways than mere geography. Once a year, typically in November, you can walk or run across it during the "Across the Bay 10K." The other 364 ½ days you drive across it. In my experience, a trip east across this bridge is best taken at sunrise and in autumn, after beach-bound traffic hurtling toward the Atlantic shore has dissipated. Once the longest continuous overwater steel structure, today this architectural wonder, by its very existence, sustains what I have come to view as the Maryland identity, a gentle balance between southern hospitality and a northeasterner's speed and edge. And the Bay Bridge is the means to achieving this balance.

For city dwellers, from the urban cultural centers of Washington DC and Baltimore, it provides the gateway to Maryland's rural Eastern Shore, a welcome and often-sought respite from daily challenges of big city and suburban life. For the farmers and fishermen of the Eastern Shore, it has become a link to broader markets and economic prosperity. Until 1953, the only means of accessing either opposite shore was via ferry, personal watercraft, or an arduous and time-consuming drive around the northern tip of the Chesapeake Bay. Today you can cross this magnificent estuary in 5 minutes.

So accompany me on a brief journey from west to east, over the bridge and beyond, a drive I take nearly every week, weather permitting. Once you have cleared the toll booths on the western shore, the sounds of your car tires rolling over the bridge joints create a quick staccato on the bridge approach, slowing to a lumbering rhythm at the bridge's crest, only to regain the accelerated cadence as you near the opposite shore. Only one lighthouse is visible from the bridge, Sandy Point Shoal Light, built in 1858 and still operational today, offering a solar-powered white light beacon at 6 second intervals and a reminder of the importance of navigational warnings.

The eastbound span rises nearly 200 feet above the bay at the highest point, curving gently from the western shore to allow for maritime traffic. The spans arch over the shipping lanes dotted with tankers and freighters, sitting just south of the bridge, awaiting entry to Baltimore's harbor, their floating parking lot sharply contrasting to the few single-masted white-sailed boats hugging the bay's edges in the distance.

The downward slope of the bridge, returns you to land, and in autumn, you are greeted with a cascade of color, foreshadowing the departure of the agricultural season. The Route 50 corridor winds east and then south and then east again, tree-lined, framed by loblolly and eastern white pine, towering red and black oaks, fast-growing poplars, dazzling maples. As you continue eastward, local produce stands punctuate the landscape, extending their season from tomatoes, sweet corn, and peaches to pumpkins and chrysanthemums, local jams and jellies. And interspersed between these family-run stands (stopovers for stocking up by day-trippers returning to the cities and suburbs) old-growth forests, sanctuary for growing herds of white-tailed deer, skirt the plowed, now fallow, fields. The deer only venture from the safety of the sheltering oaks and pines at break of day or dusk. If you scan the fields' edges, where the forest meets the plow, you can find them, often by the tens and twenties, in sharp juxtaposition to the behemoth yellow or red tractors decorating these very same fields, sitting silent, sentries awaiting the final field clearing before the hard freeze of winter.

More bridges are in your eastbound future, each an additional step away from the stress and intensity of the cities of the Western Shore: Kent Narrows, high and arched, allowing passage of boats without need for a drawbridge and providing easy access to waterfront restaurants renowned for their seafood and sunsets. The Choptank River Bridge, entry to Cambridge, brown information signs offering enticements to history and nature, to historic Christ Church or the Blackwater National Wildlife Refuge, just twelve miles south and home to resident nesting bald eagles and migrating flocks. The Nanticoke River Bridge, long and curving, skirting Vienna, its height providing views of expansive river marshes leading to the bay.

For it is the early morning hours over my years of travelling to the Eastern Shore that I treasure. Whether showering white light over the glistening marsh flats bordering the Nanticoke River or sun sparks bursting through the fog-shrouded towers of the Chesapeake Bay Bridge or the brilliant sun's inexorable climb above the Atlantic horizon, the spectacle of a new day never fails to engage the imagination. Vibrant and authoritative, painting hues of orange, red, yellow, pink and gold in ever-evolving patterns across the eastern sky only to burst into blazing brilliance overshadowing the receding colors. You must look quickly for they are gone in an instant.

And as you drive further east toward the rivers and

bays that flow into the Atlantic, make time to stop waterside to observe, along the edges of a marsh or the curve in a hidden bay, for it is at this magic brightening hour that the shorebirds engage. An osprey, often mistakenly called a "sea eagle", dips and soars, talons ready, seeking a glint of fish but disappointed in its search. A cormorant dives, repeatedly, only to eventually surface with a wriggling eel, bent on escaping an early morning fate. The eel wins out. And just as dawn breaks, the familiar armada of twelve or more buffleheads glides into the protected waters of the coastal bays and rivers. The antics of these small black and white ducks, diving into shallow waters searching for crustaceans and mollusks, only to pop up 20 seconds later, yards away from where they had entered the water, provides welcome quiet amusement.

Autumn is the time to travel east from the Bay Bridge, for as the winter draws near, throughout November and into December, the sunrises more often emerge subdued with slate grays, pale blues, more drab than silver, bringing forth field-hugging fog, delivering only the unbroken promise of eventual light.

You may have already seen the signs, "Chesapeake Country Scenic Byway", their yellow black-eyed susans enticing you to take an unplanned turn. And perhaps you have even, accidentally, navigated along portions of the carefully laid-out pathway. Once you have crossed the Chesapeake Bay Bridge, you realize why locals refer to their slice of Maryland as "God's country". Accidental travel on backroads has taken me through towns I never knew with names that hold the promise of undiscovered stories…...Reliance, Harmony, Eldorado.

I grew up in Baltimore, able to pick a mean crab by age ten and shuck an oyster by age eleven, I have travelled through 48 of the 50 states. While I love my mid-Atlantic state for its diverse geography, for its proximity to the cultures of major city centers, and for its geographical position in a weather-protected "sweet spot", relatively free from earthquakes, tornadoes, hurricanes, and paralyzing blizzards that bedevil other states, I am most grateful for the natural wonders seemingly suspended in time, once I cross the Chesapeake Bay Bridge.

I was born in Maryland. Cumberland, actually, when I had no choice of geography. Today, having lived in Connecticut, Texas, Virginia, and traveled the world, I choose Maryland.

DONNA ROTHERT is a former teacher turned corporate executive who has had a lifelong love affair with Maryland. Following career moves to Texas, Connecticut, and Virginia, and extensive global travel, she continues to explore and to write.

Crabtown

By Linda Wood

Here in Crabtown—really Annapolis, Maryland—we go bonkers over anything to do with blue crabs. We are meticulous about how we catch them, persnickety about how we cook them, and skillful at "picking" the meat from their many nooks and crannies.

We have known since childhood that crab lines are easily made with a weight and an old chicken neck tied on the end of a string. We know that a crab is on our line when it starts to stray away from the pier as the scavenger tries to take the smelly morsel to the depths of the creek. We know to very slowly pull the line inch by inch to the surface, so one of our fellow crabbers can scoop up the unsuspecting crustacean with a long-handled wire net and deposit the catch in a nearby bushel basket. And we know that our mothers have the big blue enameled crab pot waiting in the kitchen. We always steam (never boil!) them and season them with *McCormick's Old Bay* while they are cooking. At any crab feast, you'll find true crab lovers with saltine crackers and ice-cold beer close at hand. We don't mind the smell, eat them with our hands, spread our tabletops with newspaper and roll up the spoils when we are done. Some of us even call our hometown newspaper the "crab wrapper." We know to keep our trash can lids secure until garbage day, so the raccoons won't try to feast on our leftovers.

It goes without saying that we are crab cake aficionados. We use back fin or lump crab meat exclusively, with just enough filler to hold it all together, and reserve the sweeter claw meat for our famous Maryland vegetable crab soup. We like our crab cakes to be generous and fried - crisp on the outside and moist on the inside - but today we reluctantly accept more healthy broiled ones. Even though crab cakes are our favorites, a luscious crab imperial, cream of crab soup or a bubbling bowl of hot crab dip can tempt our palates as well. Our restaurants and pubs offer a mélange of Chesapeake Bay cuisine, but crab cakes always top the list.

In addition to our seafood delights, outsiders think that Crabtown *is* the United States Naval Academy, but it is much more. If an Annapolitan tells you that "George Washington slept here", believe it. He was a frequent guest of William Paca at his house on Prince George Street. Documents show that he was a familiar patron of the town taverns and is known to have lost a few shillings at the Annapolis Race Track. And he stood in the Maryland State House in 1783 to resign his commission as commander-in-chief of the Continental Army. Our State House is oldest state capitol in continuous legislative use and is the only state house ever to have served as the nation's capital.

In our rivers and creeks, boats of all shapes and sizes are moored or docked. The names on the transoms are frequently clever with their homeports indicating they have come from far and wide. We host the largest in-the-water power and sailboat shows in the United States.

Our streets are filled with old colonial homes - some majestic like the Hammond Harwood House on Maryland Avenue, but many like the row houses on Cornhill Street where the working class lived. We have outdone the other twelve original colonies in preserving our history; you'll find this at the Maryland Hall of Records here in town. Our Visitors Center refers to our town as a "museum without walls."

That history dates back to the mid 1600's when our little town was called, "Providence". It remained so until the early 1700's when the capital was moved here from St. Mary's City and Governor Sir Francis Nicholson renamed it Annapolis in honor of Princess Anne, heir to the British throne.

The United States Naval Academy - we call it The Academy and some real old-timers just call it The Yard - abuts the Historic District along with St. John's College, third oldest in the United States. No two schools could be further apart in their curricula, their objectives and their students. However, they do engage in a spirited croquet competition each spring. But here in Annapolis, we are, first and foremost, lacrosse fans. Kids, both girls and boys, carry lacrosse sticks around like earlier generations carried baseball gloves. However, we do take time out to cheer with gusto for Navy football, especially when they play Army.

I am a born and raised Annapolitan. So, when the literary experts said, "write what you know", you can see that the obvious setting for my story was my hometown. My thoughts are scattered among the brick sidewalks, the endless history, the colonial buildings, and the waterways and bridges. And I have sprinkled my memories in real places - places I know - some like my own backyard. Those of you who live here in Crabtown could walk with me on the familiar streets, both of today and yesterday. If you don't live here, you are going to want to visit.

No book about Crabtown would be complete without some expert direction on how to make a real Maryland crab cake. The master can only be my grandmother, a born and bred Annapolitan. I have fond memories of her standing in the kitchen shredding a piece of day-old bread between her hands. Fine homemade crumbs were the filler for a pound of crabmeat along with a few spices, a little mayonnaise and an egg to hold it all together. If you find yourself in a restaurant <u>outside</u> the Maryland area, and the menu says "Real Maryland Crab Cakes" - beware! Unless the chef is from our area, you are going to be really disappointed. So, come visit and get the real thing.

Grandmother Ruth's Crab Cakes

1 lb of backfin or lump crab meat
1 slice of day-old bread made into fine crumbs (rub between hands)
1 large egg - beaten
¼ cup of mayonnaise
1 tsp. Worcestershire sauce
1 tsp. dry mustard
1 Tbs. <u>Old Bay Seasoning</u> - more or less to taste

Carefully remove any shell bits from crab meat - you do not want to break up any lumps. Add all ingredients in a large bowl and mix carefully. Gently form into cakes and fry in hot oil or broil. Depending on the size of cakes, it should make about eight. Serve with tartar sauce if desired, but most Annapolitans eat them plain or on saltine crackers. They are good hot or cold.

In my house crab cake dinners were always accompanied by fresh local tomato slices, potato salad, cole slaw and sometimes french fries. Bon appétit!

Once Upon a Dream in Maryland
by Linda Wood

Once upon a time, there was a little eight-year-old boy who thought his most prized possession was his lacrosse stick and the most exciting thing he could do was "make the team". After he did just that, the most important thing he could do was "play". His legs looked like toothpicks in the wide legged gym shorts and when he tucked in his shirt, his number disappeared into his pants. He doted on every word the coach said and his mother had to rope and tie him in order to get his jersey off of his body and into the washing machine.

His first coach was a former Johns Hopkins All-American and this little boy played on what that coach called his "Jet Set Midfield". Coach used that term to indicate enthusiasm, because whenever he yelled for them, they moved like little jets to get their chance on the field. This little boy was the center middie and his two partners were his brother and his best friend. They were the youngest members of the team that year so their playing time was limited. But when they did get chance, they played with such gusto that the coach could not help but notice. They were constantly trying to emulate the older boys when they cradled the ball in their sticks, zigzagged through the defense and took a shot at the goal, He was hoping to put it in the upper left corner where the goalie might have a hard time seeing it. How many hours he practiced that shot. His mother once told him that if he could run down the field in the rain, and put that little ball in the upper corner of the goal, she could not understand how he could stand over top of the laundry hamper and miss.

Over the years as his skill level changed, so did his dreams. His high school years were very successful, yet he still wanted more. He knew he wanted to play for a Division I team and capture the NCAA Championship. He was not unique. There are thousands of little boys out there hoping that someday they might have the opportunity. But few get the chance.

Ten years and scores of games later that same little boy walked out onto the field in a Johns Hopkins University jersey. He not only made the team, but he was one of the three starting attackmen. It was an accomplishment in itself, since he was only a freshman. His legs were no longer skinny, his shoulders were broad, and when he tucked in his shirt, his favorite number showed bold and proud for all to see. To say he was excited would be an understatement. He thought about all the years he had played getting to this point and all the friends he had made along the way. He thought how badly he wanted one more memory.

When Hopkins came to Annapolis to play Navy, another little boy, much like the little boy he used to be, came up to him and said, "If you win the national championship, can I have your stick?" He remembered asking the same question himself to one of his lacrosse heroes years ago. It was a common practice. He was flattered so he told him, "If we both find ourselves at the championship game, the stick is yours."

The season progressed and with each win he got one step further down the road to that coveted moment of being in the Final Four. He wondered if it was all possible. It's a long season and it was important to take it one game at a time. He knew that if you looked ahead, sometimes there isn't a tomorrow.

The day final arrived and now the grownup little boy was at the threshold of living his dream. His team won the semifinal. They been ranked number one in the seedings and lived up to their expectations. The noise level was deafening as the teams came out of their locker rooms and onto the field. The stadium was overflowing with fans from all over the East Coast – the hotbed of lacrosse.

He knew his father was in the stands pacing back and forth as much as possible. He knew would have taken something for his traditional pre-game tension headache; perhaps even a double dose today. And his mother would be glued to her seat, wearing the black and blue team colors and hardly moving a muscle until the game was over.

As they went through their warmup drills, the thought of where he was and how much this game meant to him and his teammates was ever present in his mind. It seemed an eternity before the referee blew the whistle to start the game. He heard the roar from the crowd and felt his heart pounding. But he knew that he would be alright once the game got underway. He always was.

Hopkins won the first face off, maintained possession of the ball and he personally put the first score on the board. The crowd went wild. His teammates followed with several more goals in quick succession. But Syracuse dug in their heels and added point to their side of the scoreboard. The tension was building with every pass, every save, every shot, every fast break and every score. Halftime came and went and although Hopkins maintained a lead, it was slim at most.

"Can we really hold on, can we do it?" he thought.

But as the fourth quarter was winding down, they were but one point ahead. He looked up at the clock and saw that there were only a few seconds left and he knew. He knew that the championship was theirs, because he had the ball in his stick and he knew he could keep it away from the Orangemen. The fans harmoniously counted down the last ten seconds and the most exhilarating feeling swept over him as he realized his long-time dream – his team won the national championship – the highest honor in college lacrosse – and he was part of it. He threw his helmet into the air, dropped his gloves somewhere and shouted with his teammates, "We did it, we did it!" They all jumped up and down, hugged each other and shed a few unashamed tears.

He knew his parents and friends were somewhere in the overwhelming crowd, anxious to offer their congratulations and share his joy. But security was so tight, he knew they would never be able to get onto the field. He would celebrate with them later. The clapping and the cheering continued and in the midst of all the fervor, he felt a tug on his jersey. He looked down to see the face of a little boy who had somehow eluded the security guards.

"Do you remember me?"

Of course, he remembered. He saw himself ten years ago. He picked up his well-worn stick with the perfect pocket and handed it to the little boy and said, "Sure, I remember you. I hope it helps you realize one of your dreams. It sure helped me get mine today." The little boy walked off the field clutching the stick like it was his most prized possession – a gift from a young man who used to think it was only a dream to win the national championship.

This might a story about a particular young man, but it is a story about all those athletes out there who are now or used to be little boys with dreams, no matter what the sport. Some of them are lucky enough to have their dream come true. All of them a lucky enough to have the dreams in the first place.

What happened to the little boy in the story whose dreams came true? Today he coaches little boys with dreams, including his own sons. Perhaps they, too, will have their dreams come true, whatever they are.

LINDA WOOD was born and raised in Annapolis and currently resides there. Crabtown is the frequent setting for many of her short stories. As a wife of 55+ years, a mother of two creatively mischievous boys, grandmother of five precious angels and being blessed with a myriad of fascinating and unusual friends, there is much about which to write.

Muskrat Love
By Bronwyn Mitchell-Strong

In South Dorchester County, Maryland, the measure of a man or woman is literally taken in skins. .

As the legend goes, two men set about one day talking about muskrat skinning. One or the other or both threw a gauntlet, and a competition was born. From those humble beginnings grew forth what is now the National Outdoor Show hosted each year in Golden Hill, MD, population 123, where the World Champion Muskrat Skinning Champion is crowned.

Each February, for 74 years now, save for the two years the Show was cancelled due to WWII, the National Outdoor Show has celebrated the outdoor lifestyle lived in the lowland marshes of Maryland's Eastern Shore, including oystering and crabbing, log sawing, duck and goose calling, game cooking demonstrations, and local beauty pageants, and skinning.

Dorchester County is located on the Eastern Shore of Maryland. The state of Maryland, whose perimeter was seemingly drawn by a drunken cartographer, is almost completely bisected by the Chesapeake Bay. The divide isn't merely geographical. For most of its existence, Maryland's Eastern Shore, part of the Delmarva Peninsula, comprised mostly of Delaware, with a piece each of Virginia and Maryland, was geographically isolated from the "mainland."

The land is a coastal plain, flat and dominated by

farmland and marshes. Only 8% of the state's population call the Eastern Shore home. And most of the locals prefer it that way. A favorite bumper sticker reads, "There is no life west of the Chesapeake Bay."

It wasn't until 1952 that the first bridge crossing the Bay was constructed. Before then, if you wanted to get to Delmarva or the Atlantic Ocean, you were forced to circumnavigate the Bay from the north. Then and now, most of the traffic over the Bay Bridge has one destination in mind, the beach, passing unaware through some of the most beautiful and fragile landscapes Maryland has to offer.

While the Western Shore boasts the biggest towns and cities, the first county seat in Maryland was actually founded on the eastern shore on Kent Island.

Humans have always tended to settle in areas where the living is good. Before the English, the region was home to many tribes of Native Americans. With plentiful stores of wildlife and fisheries, the eastern shore lands offer a bounty of goodness for its tenants—fish, fur, forest, and fertile soils for agriculture—there for the taking by those ready to put in some hard, honest work. Slackers and slickers need not apply.

It was 2005. I was living and working on the Eastern Shore of Maryland, transplanted from New Orleans via Botswana, Dallas, and American Samoa, when I first learned about The National Outdoor Show from some folks working for the US Fish and Wildlife Service.

The moment I learned about The Show, I knew that I had to go. The date of the show was approaching so I began to search for additional information to help organize my visit and to use to bait friends to accompany me.

Typing in all manner of search criteria on Google, I received only the basic amount of information—date and location. Frustrated, I picked up the phone and physically dialed the Dorchester County Tourism Office. While the woman on the line was very pleasant, she was unable to give me any more information than date and time. She did give me the number of a woman who would be able to fill me on the specifics I so desired. I called and left a message.

Two days later, a woman named Virginia returned my call and with a deep shore accent—and a boatload of patience—tried to answer my questions. I wanted to know the exact schedule of events. Virginia explained that the gates opened at 11 a.m., but the skinning didn't start until afternoon and wouldn't likely finish until midnight or the a.m. She encouraged me to arrive early for the exhibits, food and other competitions, insisting that there was enough to keep people busy all day.

I invited the one friend who I knew wouldn't be able to refuse an invitation to a muskrat skinning competition. Traveling over from "the mainland," the Western Shore, she arrived late with her son and his friend, both six years old. As the sun set, we drove to Golden Hill on open roads that wound through fields, travelled over water and seemingly floated over the top of the marsh grasses.

With a name like the Outdoor Show, I advised everyone to dress for an evening outdoors. Bundled from head to toe, we entered the elementary school to pay our entrance fee. It didn't take long to realize that the entire outdoor show was in fact held indoors. I assumed that skinning, shucking oysters and log cutting, all competitions featured in the show, were activities that were better done outdoors. While this may be true in reality, an outdoor set-up is not optimal for an audience's enjoyment. So one week prior to the festival, students at the South Dorchester Elementary and Middle School are let out of class while the entire school is transformed in preparation for the show.

The classrooms are cleared of desks and chairs to make room for the variety of displays from the police, Coast Guard, and national wildlife refuges—and the many vendors selling everything from plastic toys, carved wildlife art, live ducks, and t-shirts to arts and crafts. In the gym/auditorium, a wooden runway is erected. An area of the hallway is reserved for the muskrat cooking competition. The kitchen is outfitted with a cash register, the milk and juice boxes replaced with soda, and the offerings of pizza and tater tots replaced with a menu of crab cakes and oyster fritters.

Blending in was not an option. It wasn't just the arctic gear we were wearing that gave us away. While we were pegged for outsiders the moment we stepped inside, we were eagerly accepted as part of the fold, and left as old friends.

We took our time maneuvering through the displays perusing the goods, being assured over and over that the goods were handmade in the USA while the kids ran from booth to booth collecting candy and trinkets. When hunger took over, we went looking for a muskrat sandwich.

Unfortunately, the muskrat ladies, having just run out of rats, had packed up their portable kitchen in preparation for the show. Crestfallen that we couldn't partake of the regional specialty, we headed into the cafeteria and had to "settle" for crabs and oysters, opting for the oyster fritter, a conglomeration of 5-6 good sized oysters fried in a slightly sweet fluffy batter served between two slices of white bread, a more than respectable second choice. Sitting at the table, I was finally able to read through the program we received upon admission. I learned that a portion of the money collected at the door, through the auctions and from the sale of food at this event is filtered back into the community through the National Outdoor Show Foundation in the form of scholarships and grants. I ordered another fritter.

I learned also that each year, the show is dedicated to a member of the community who best exemplifies the spirit of the show. This year the show saluted the late Inez Abbott—of the muskrat skinning contest in 1970 and 1971. The remainder of the program highlighted the previous year winners of the pageants and various contests, acknowledged contributors and presented the schedule of events. As Virginia explained on the phone, the show does have something for everyone.

Friday is the Miss Outdoor Show pageant, while Saturday plays hosts to everything else. Saturday morning, local children compete for the junior pageant titles. The afternoon is full of demonstrations and competitions including, muskrat cooking, duck carving, gun dog demonstrations, and duck/goose/turkey calling. If you want to sample muskrat dishes, you have to arrive early on Saturday because, as the program explained, they are available until "find out when" which translates to, "for a limited time only."

The Saturday evening show, which consists of the skinning, shucking and log-cutting competitions, auction, and awards ceremony, begins at 7 p.m. and finishes when it finishes. There was no ending time printed in the program, and this was not an error.

Chatting with a Show regular over a Coke and an oyster fritter, we learned that it was important to grab a seat early. Heeding the advice, we headed into the auditorium around 6:30 pm and found four empty seats only two rows from the stage. Fifteen minutes later, the auditorium was packed, and it was standing room only out in the halls. Then the emcee for the evening came out to announce that the bridge to Hooper Island was up. With a few folks stuck on the island side on their way to the show, we would be starting a bit late.

The program began with a salute to the pageant winners from Friday night who promenaded up and down the runway, followed by the oyster races. As sessile bivalves, oysters are not the speediest of creatures. But the race does not pit oyster to oyster but rather kids against the clock to see how fast they can harvest oysters hidden in a sand-laden baby pool. To make things more interesting, the kids have to dress for the task by donning a pair of oil skins, boots, and gloves before harvesting.

Oysters are indeed in a race against time and circumstance. Two hundred years ago, there were enough oysters living in the Chesapeake Bay to filter the entire volume of the Bay in two weeks. Today, with populations decimated through overfishing, disease, decreased water quality and habitat loss, the same filtering takes more than a year. At this rate of decline, it is unlikely that the kids participating in the oyster race will get to put on the oil skins as adults and tong oysters as their ancestors have done.

Once the oyster races were over, the baby pool was dragged off the stage and replaced with a pole and a wooden scaffold and the atmosphere began to buzz with anticipation—the skinning was about to begin. Raccoon skinning was up first.

The animals used in the competition are not provided to the competitors. Competitors must bring their own. The fresher the kill, the easier the skinning. However, according to the rules, kills cannot be made less than two hours before show time. All animals are inspected and locked up before the competition begins, and re-inspected before they are taken to the stage. The emcee reminisced with decided glee about the year when one of the muskrats, not quite dead, jumped into the crowd. Good thing the possum isn't valued for its skin. The pole used to hold the coons is the same one used to hold up the school's volleyball. I learned that it has been used as part of the competition for at least the past ten years and is much reviled by the students after the show despite the liberal use of disinfectant.

Coon skinners have their choice of pole or scaffold. Once the animals are securely trussed up by one or two legs, depending upon personal style, the emcee announces, "hands off." Then with one hand deftly holding a knife, and the other fluttering anxiously in the wind, the skinners wait for the time honored—"Ready, Set, Skin!"

At "skin," the action begins with cuts and maneuvers passed down from generation to generation. When compared to the other "skinnables," raccoons seemed to be the most stubborn, requiring the greatest amount of brawn as evidenced by the skinners' contorted faces and flexed muscles as they leveraged the weight of their entire bodies to pull the skin away from the carcasses.

As with any sport, the crowd plays its part—cheering, motivating, guiding, coaching. This being the first match of the evening and first in my life's experience, the shouts from the crowd left a lasting impression "cut, cut cut," "stop cutting," "pull," "you're pulling its head off—stop—you're pulling its head off." .

Halfway through the first round of coon skinning, my friend and I turned to the kids to gauge their feelings. They both announced that they were fine. We were not sure if this was a good or bad but decided to stick it out.

The competitors are not alone on the stage. Each one is surrounded by a minimum of three timers. Yet timing is but one aspect of the skinning competition. The finished skins must be of market quality. Therefore, once the skins are fully removed, the times are marked and then the skins are pulled over several judge's outstretched arms one by one—inside out. The underside of the skin is visible to both judge and crowd in a "Silence of the Lambs" sort of manner, and checked for nicks and holes, for which deductions are assessed.

Contestants will be disqualified if he or she does not leave both eye holes in the muskrat hide.

Contestants will be disqualified if he or she does not leave the nose of the muskrat in the hide.

Contestants will be disqualified if he or she has any knife cuts in the hide.

Contestants will be disqualified if he or she pulls either of the hides apart.

Contestants will be disqualified if he or she leaves either foot on hide.

Contestants will be disqualified if he or she touches muskrat hides or carcasses before the judges have completed judging the contest.

Once the skinning started, it didn't take long for the heated auditorium to take on a special fragrance. For a while, it was manageable, then a line was crossed. After almost losing my oyster fritter right there in the second row, I spied a coconut flavor lip balm hanging from a cord around one of the kid's neck. I was thankfully granted permission to and then proceeded to slather the balm all over my nose and into my nostrils, the rest of our group quickly following suit.

After the coons, came the nutria.

Nutria are a semi-aquatic rodent native to South

America that were brought to the U.S. in the 1800's to bolster the fur trade. After the collapse of the fur industry, with no natural predators, nutria populations exploded. The problem is that nutria consume 25% of their body weight of 14 pounds daily in marsh grasses, from the root, causing a significant loss of valuable wetlands. . The nutria also out-compete their native cousins, the muskrat, for food and habitat.

Nutria have been found in 17 states nationwide, Maryland serving as the most northern. Building no dens, during a cold snap, nutria populations plummet. But it only takes a few to build back up populations.

Being from New Orleans, I was all too acquainted with nutria. To help curb the nutria problem, the state decided to create a new market for the animal. Building on the state's culinary reputation, grants were distributed to chefs to develop world class recipes to create a food craze. While nutria dishes can be found on some menus, it never reached the desired fever pitch. A bounty of $4 per nutria tail is paid out to hunters in Louisiana where there is no limit, and every day is open to nutria hunting.

In Maryland, with a pretty defined geographic area of habitation, the Eastern Shore, the Federal Government, took a different tact. In 2002, working hand in hand with the state and local governments, and local residents, the ambitious goal of eradicating all nutria from Delmarva was set. Using local knowledge combined with GPS, the marshes were systematically trapped and re-trapped and re-trapped until every single nutria was eventually dispatched. As of 2016, all of the known nutria populations have been removed from over a quarter million acres of the Delmarva Peninsula, and the Chesapeake Bay Nutria Eradication Project is implementing efforts to verify eradication and remove residual animals. In 2005, the program was in full swing, nutria were prevalent, and therefore a natural addition to The Outdoor Show.

To prepare the stage for nutria skinning, the pole and scaffold were removed, and the freshly mopped stage, used at other times of the year for music classes, school plays and pep rallies, was covered with flattened cardboard boxes.

Nutria skinners worked from a kneeling position. And unlike with the raccoons, the contestants, prior to the start of the competition, set about massaging the animals, loosening the skin from the bones—an oddly sensual ritual.

After the nutria came the main event, muskrats, the smallest of the three animals, the biggest draw, holding the most prestige. Instead of skinning one animal, as was the practice with both coons and nutria, in the muskrat category, three rats are skinned in the semifinals and five in the finals. For muskrats, categories include men, women, beginner and junior. The family that skins together, stays together.

Because of their small size (1-4 pounds), muskrats are handled differently than the other two skinned species. After a quick cut to the hind section, the entire animal is turned inside out on itself. This happens in one move, accompanied by the rather unnerving sound of cracking bones. At this point, the animal is reduced to a sphere with an inside out skin covering. Then, with a few more cuts and a couple of tugs, the skin cleanly separated from the body.

The action is fast and furious. Like the four-minute mile, people dream of the five-muskrat minute. This year, during the frenzy of the round, one competitor accidentally threw the skin onto a member of the audience instead of the floor beside her—both were nonplussed.

When it was the women's turn, the reigning Miss Outdoors Show was not going to let a ball gown and tiara stop her from competing. After a quick wardrobe change, she emerged on the stage ready to do battle. Unfortunately, she had to withdraw from the competition after cutting herself on the first rat.

It was 11 p.m. before the skinning competitions finished, but the night was far from over. Oyster shucking, log cutting, and the awards ceremony were all waiting in the wings. Virginia wasn't lying when she said the Show lasted well into the night. We, however, didn't.

With the smell of dead muskrat clinging to our clothes, we hit the road home. In the car, the mainland kids picked up their game boys, my mainland friend waited impatiently for the cell service to return to her phone, and this Eastern Shore transplant dreamed of becoming the next World Muskrat Skinning Champion. It's an Eastern Shore thing. You wouldn't understand.

BROMWYN MITCHELL-STRONG: Born on the bayous of Louisiana, Bronwyn has lived in Botswana, on the island of American Samoa, Dallas, Texas, and three different cities in Maryland working mainly in the fields of environmental protection and education. Bronwyn's writing is pulled from her experiences traveling, living abroad, and her quest to do everything at least once.

Fireballs, Tsunamis, Volcanoes—Oh My!

By Edna Troiano

What's to love about Maryland? It's right in the name—the land. In a geographically small state, Marylanders can enjoy the Atlantic Ocean, the Chesapeake Bay, and historically and geographically important rivers. Hikers can walk forty miles of the Appalachian Trail, climb Sugarloaf Mountain, or walk through nature preserves and parks. Lovers of city life can enjoy Baltimore, aptly named Charm City, or they can step across the border into our nation's capital. If they look upward, they can spot over four hundred species of birds, including those passing through on one of the country's major flyways. With all there is to see and do, they may neglect to look down and ponder the spectacular events that formed the land.

The Maryland shore, mecca to so many vacationers, was created by plate tectonics—the slow movement of rigid plates drifting over the earth's mantle. Once part of the supercontinent Pangaea, the Maryland shore emerged between 3 and 3.5 billion years ago as large plates slowly drifted over the earth's mantle. As the huge landmass split apart, what is now West Africa broke away from the Atlantic seaboard, gradually leaving behind the beaches Marylanders so love.

The Chesapeake Bay, the largest estuary in the United States, is fed by over 150 rivers and streams. Home to over three hundred species of fish and shell fish, the bay also attracts dolphins and even the occasional whale as well as a wide array of wildlife. Marylanders are familiar with the bay's role in industry, ecology, and tourism, but few know the remarkable story of the cataclysmic event that contributed to its formation. Over thirty-five million years ago, a bolide—a large exploding fireball—traveling 70,000 miles an hour crashed into what was then a shallow, offshore part of the Atlantic.

The bolide, one to three miles wide, formed a huge impact crater over fifty miles wide and about a mile deep—almost as deep as the Grand Canyon, in what is now near the mouth of the Chesapeake Bay. On impact, rocks, sediment, and water soared into the air, and a tsunami roared over the land, reaching as far as the Blue Ridge Mountains. The land, which had been a tropical rain forest, was now a shallow warm sea.

The walls of the crater gradually slumped in, and sediment settled over the area. It was not until 1983 that scientists discovered the crater—the largest known in the country—that had existed for millions of years.

Although glaciers of the last ice age didn't reach Maryland, they still had a major impact on the land. About 20,000 years ago, a mile-thick glacier reached as far as southern Pennsylvania. As the climate warmed and the glacier gradually began to retreat, the sea level rose, and meltwater ran down river beds and created new channels. About 10,000 years ago, rising sea water entered the Susquehanna river valley and mingled with meltwater from the rivers, creating the Bay.

The Susquehanna, the longest river on the East Coast, meanders for 464 miles before emptying into the Chesapeake Bay. Dated 320 to 340 million years ago, it also has the distinction of being among the world's oldest rivers, older even than some of the mountains it flows by. The Potomac, a mere 405 miles long, ranks as the fourth longest river on the Eastern Seaboard. It's also younger, with its age estimated from as little as two to as much as twenty million years. The gradual rising of the mountains in Western Maryland coupled with the more recent meltwaters of the glacier contributed to the current shape of the Susquehanna, the Potomac, and other Maryland rivers.

On the western shore of the Bay in Calvert County, a twenty-four mile stretch of cliffs, aptly named Calvert Cliffs, attracts fossils hunters who easily pick up sharks' teeth, sometimes including those of the giant Megalodon, as well as a variety of plant and animal fossils. The eroding cliffs have exposed the bones of whales, fish, seals, and sea turtles. Rarer finds include the remains of mastodons, camels, and crocodiles. For much of the early Paleozoic era (542-251 million years ago) much of Maryland was covered by a shallow sea. As the sea receded, wind and waves eroded the shore and the cliffs were exposed. Although people associate fossils with the cliffs, all the land once covered by the sea contains similar fossils. Dig deep enough, and the fossil bed will appear everywhere the sea once lay.

For those more attracted to mountains than to waterways, Maryland offers a spectacular array in the Appalachian and Blue Ridge Mountains. Of course, none of those mountains would exist without plate tectonics. The separation of plates created the Maryland shore, but when plates collide the opposite effect occurs—land is forced upward. The Appalachian Mountains in Western Maryland arose 480 million years ago. The evidence that plates collided is found in volcanic rocks, marine sediment, and even traces of an ancient sea floor elevated from their original place. East of the Appalachians, the Blue Ridge, although part of the Appalachians, are older—dating from as much as 1.1 billion years ago, making them among the world's oldest mountains. The Blue Ridge Mountains consist mostly of volcanic formations, reflecting yet more long-ago cataclysmic events.

The next time you're at the shore, on the rivers, hiking through the forests, or looking up at a bald eagle or great blue heron soaring overhead, take a minute to look down and think about the ripping apart and butting together of tectonic plates, the fireball and tsunami, the glacier, and the volcanic action and erosion that over millions of years created the land you're standing on.

EDNA M. TROIANO: After retiring from the College of Southern Maryland, switched from academic to popular writing. Her magazine articles, essays, book reviews, and poems have been widely published. Her latest book is a biography of Josiah Henson.

Welcome to Maryland
By Jane Newhagen

Marylanders, there's an alien in your midst, undetected, since I look pretty much like you or someone you know. I'm a migrant from Florida to Maryland and I'm here to stay. I read that people like me are called "halfbacks," folks who started in the north, went way south, and ultimately wound up here in the mid-Atlantic. Well, I may be halfway back, but I'm certainly not halfhearted about it. I'm learning my way around.

Here, the leaves change and fall in the loveliest way and when they're wet and slippery on the streets I can practice up for winter driving. What snow there is falls at a measured pace, at least most of the time. Just enough to close the schools and cancel meetings, but the power stays on—ordinarily, anyway. Ice? Well, no place is perfect, is it?

And the summers! I've heard Marylanders complain about three consecutive days of heat and humidity! Do you know the dreaded h & h starts in May in Florida and doesn't let up until November? I've got it good here. And there's spring. Daffodils and crocus, azaleas and rhododendrons greet the lengthening and warming days with a seemingly spontaneous display. It's even possible to forget the damp chill of kneeling in the October garden to plant the bulbs!

There's a festival of horticulture here! Liriope and bird of paradise grow next to maples and oaks. I'd better like crape myrtle; it's everywhere. Who isn't delighted by the pinks and reds as they burst into bloom? And who, by the end of summer, isn't just a little relieved when those long-lived blossoms give way to another palette?

That's all superficial. I judge a place, just as a person, by its character rather than its looks. Maryland is characterized by its generosity. Look how she gave land for our country's capital city. She's reliable; she didn't take back the gift like Virginia did. She's loyal. Maryland didn't secede from the union during the War Between the States. Is it true that Lincoln had several pro-slavery politicians arrested in order to guarantee that result? Admirable and complex, like a good, lasting friend.

And Maryland is right in the middle of things politically, geographically, and culturally. Stretching to the west, mountains, rivers, and tranquil vistas beckon. Sandy beaches, seaports, and crabs draw me in the other direction. She boasts the second star in the contest for horse racing's Triple Crown. There are over a dozen symphony orchestras, myriad galleries, and over 200 cemeteries in this state. Birthplace of notables like Thurgood Marshall, Rachel Carson, Spiro Agnew, Frederick Douglas, John Bolton, and Harriet Tubman, I get the sense that I'm swirling in a kaleidoscope of history and current events. And this snuggling up against the capital city will be both a cultural blessing, a boon for the political activist in me, and a traffic trial unless I just stay off the roads when everybody is rushing to be somewhere other than where they are.

Maryland, here I am and this isn't some replay of that 1970s hit Stuck in the Middle with You. I may have settled in the middle, but I'm not making any concessions and I'm certainly not stuck. Rather, I've found a place that seems to offer the best of many worlds. I think Maryland is a Middle Way, a path balanced between extremes and offering a scenic road for me to travel for the foreseeable future.

JANE NEWHAGEN grew up in Denver, graduated from Brown University, and has lived up and down the east coast of the U.S.; Paris, France, and Key West. She recently moved to Silver Spring, MD. Her three historical novels, *Sand Dollar, Pieces of Eight*, and *Chambered Nautilus* are tales of old Key West.

Celebrating Crab Mechanics

By Donna Rothert

My colleague Susan was moving from California to the East Coast. During two years of working for a defense contractor, she in California and I in Maryland, we had become fast friends, meeting regularly at our Boston headquarters. I couldn't wait, eager to introduce her to "my" Maryland.

While I compiled a list of places to go and things to see, Susan, a self-proclaimed CrossFit buff and "foodie", insisted that restaurants be at the top of our "How To Make Susan Feel at Home in Maryland" list. So just three days after her arrival, her unpacked boxes sitting ignored in her rental apartment, we headed for Mike's just south of Annapolis for her first sally into the storied Maryland tradition of "The Crab Feast."

You see during our travels together those two years, Susan had learned to tolerate my vocal frustration when confronted with a menu item highlighted as "Maryland Crabcakes." From Texas to California, she had watched me warn unwitting wait staff that I carried a Maryland driver's license as well as a Maryland birth certificate. So in her mind, our first Maryland meal undoubtedly had to be crabs.

Susan watched as the waitress at Mike's unceremoniously emptied the tray of twelve steamed blue crabs onto our paper-draped table, turning to me with mild alarm. "Okaaaaaaaaay… Now what do I do?" Fair question from my colleague who was native to Illinois and had spent her last eight years in Los Angeles.

I welcomed her plaintive query. As a youngster, I had spent many summers on Maryland's bay and ocean shores, tying chicken necks to lines and wading into sandy, shallow, clear waters to scoop up the lone crab that had taken the bait. Or under the direction of my second cousins, I had baited a wire crab pot with chicken necks or cat food or fish heads and waited impatiently for hours to see what the river or bay had given up. By the time I was seven, I had completed what I believe to be an important Maryland rite of passage. Using a long-poled, wood-handled crab net, I ensnared a freshly-captured crab as it scooted haphazardly across the dock and then I gingerly, very gingerly, grabbed that live blue crab by its back two flippers, safe from its outsized claws. Success! With that memory still fresh, I fully appreciated Susan's foreboding upon first encountering a blue crab. To non-Marylanders it seems not to matter whether it is freshly-pulled from the bay waters or has already been steamed and dumped inelegantly in the middle of a brown-paper-covered table.

This fear of the blue crab, the "beautiful swimmer" of the Chesapeake Bay, is legitimate. Alive, it skitters sideways when seized and brought to land, making it impossible to anticipate its line of attack. Its large, outsized pincers extend menacingly as it prepares to defend itself from capture. Its hard impenetrable shell is baffling to young and old. And to further detract from any appeal, it is partially blue, a color rarely found on our dinner plates or in our grocery baskets.

Yet to Maryland natives or those hardy souls willing to take a chance, the blue crab offers two rewards. First, as a succulent seafood delicacy, hard-won after tedious and at times bewildering dismantling of its shell. And second, as justification for hours of lively camaraderie at waterside settings in what has become a traditional Maryland summertime event, "The Crab Feast."

Participation in "The Crab Feast" requires diligence and dexterity and, let's face it, crab picking is not for the squeamish or faint of heart. But Susan was game. After the once lively and fearsome blue crab had been steamed, its shell now a bright orange, she was faced with the intimidating task of actually acquiring the delectable meat known as back fin.

Admittedly, contradictory advice is often offered to the novice crab-picker. Friends and family often spar heatedly over the best possible approach to "picking" a crab. Wash off the remnants of Old Bay and start with a smooth, clean outer shell or dig into the crab immediately, hoping your hands have no small cuts susceptible to the tangy spice? Remove the claws first or wait until the hard pointed outer shell has been removed? Use a sharp knife to cut through the nautilus-like chambers or squash the crab between your hand and a hard surface fracturing the walls of cartilage?

Then, once you gain the back fin does it go straight to your lips? Or do you dip each morsel into the smoothness of melted butter? Or like an Eastern Shore native, do you dip in the tang of apple cider vinegar? And finally, perhaps the most important question of all, do you eat as you go or do you steadily pick your allotment of crabs, creating an ever-growing stockpile of crabmeat, waiting to enjoy the harvest of your labor all at once? Susan remained undeterred.

I explained that even within my own family, there are disparate philosophies of crab picking. My older son Adam is a build-your-pyramid, delayed-gratification champion. He will pick six or more crabs straight, knife at the ready, slicing and snipping, donating all claws to a communal pile, nesting the empty shells, one on top of the other, before sweeping them into the at-ready trashcan. Only then, hands washed, working area clear, will he polish off his pyramid of pure, glistening, sweet, back fin crab meat. He is a much sought-after guest because he finds joy not just in the consumption but also in the efficiency of the process. In the unlikely event there are uneaten crabs, he will happily pick those remaining, producing the meat for next day crabcakes or crab dip.

On the other hand, my younger son Andrew is an eat-as-you-go advocate. While both start the process with the removal of the crab "apron", followed by the quick twist of the wrist to remove the carapace, their paths then diverge. Adam immediately removes claws, flippers, and internal organs to then better conduct the search for the back fin without distraction. Andrew, by contrast, will first leave the crab relatively intact, pausing to wield his mallet swiftly and accurately to unlock and savor the easily-accessible claw meat before beginning his search for the back fin.

Beginners also differ in their responses to the process. Mary, a colleague from a career stint in Dallas, had visited me over the summer. While willing to try my freshly-prepared crabcakes, she fled the kitchen, dismayed to observe the decimation of the crab while I picked through the smaller chambers to acquire the desirable back fin. By contrast, Susan, on this first trip to Mike's, attacked the process with an analytical energy and enthusiasm that earned her immediate honorary Marylander status. After one crab and minimal instruction, she was a pro.

And as we proceeded to demolish our dozen medium-sized crabs, it occurred to me that perhaps the most appealing element of crab picking is "The Crab Feast" itself, usually conducted in the heat of summer, often waterside at restaurants or homes close to the actual bounty of the bay or river. Rarely do Marylanders pick crabs alone. It is not a solitary process. This feast is informal and messy, often loud and raucous, and always laughter-filled. Utensils are limited to wooden mallets and sharp knives. Plates are notable by their absence and large rolls of paper towels replace napkins. Generous sheets of brown paper substitute for a tablecloth. Trash bags or trash cans often sit on the floor at the table corners, ready for frequent removal of shells to make room for continued crab picking. Beer is the beverage of choice. And all are welcome, young and old, athlete and couch potato, beginning picker or experienced pro, through trial and error, all refining their own system, proceeding at their own pace, and finally, achieving their own rhythm, rewarded with the sweet delicacy of the blue crab. Sometimes coleslaw and corn on the cob accompany the main dish, but the celebrity is the blue crab.

So as my friend Susan would attest, if you have not experienced a crab feast in Maryland on a hot summer's day, seek out an invitation or gather friends and head for a seafood joint recommended by the locals. Proximity to the water is not required, but always enhances the experience. Prepare for occasional frustration, fun-filled conversation, and the eventual reward of the sweet meat of the blue crab. You will not be disappointed.

DONNA ROTHERT is a former teacher turned corporate executive who has had a lifelong love affair with Maryland. Following career moves to Texas, Connecticut, and Virginia, and extensive global travel, she continues to explore and to write.

Autumn, Crossing the Chesapeake

By Donna Rothert

How can anyone treasure a bridge? I do. And along with the Maryland state flag and the blue crab, this bridge that I treasure is an often-recognized symbol of the state of Maryland.

As I see it, the Chesapeake Bay Bridge sustains the Maryland identity, a gentle balance between southern hospitality and a northeasterner's speed and edge. Opened in 1952 and expanded in 1973, its 4.3 miles of steel and concrete join two geographical halves of Maryland in more ways than mere geography. Once the longest continuous overwater steel structure, today this architectural wonder sustains this identity, allowing for easy cultural and economic commerce, between urban and pastoral, progress and tradition, urgency and stillness.

Once a year, typically in November, you can walk or run across it during the "Across the Bay 10K." The other 364 ½ days you speed across it. A trip east across this bridge is best taken at sunrise and in autumn, after beach-bound traffic hurtling toward the Atlantic shore has dissipated. For city dwellers, from the urban cultural centers of Washington and Baltimore, it provides the gateway to Maryland's rural Eastern Shore, a welcome and often-sought respite from daily challenges of big city and suburban life. For the farmers and fishermen of the Eastern Shore, it has become a link to broader markets and economic prosperity. Until 1952, the only means of accessing either shore was via ferry, personal watercraft, or an arduous and time-consuming drive around the northern tip of the Chesapeake Bay. Today you can cross this magnificent estuary that is the Chesapeake in five minutes.

So, accompany me on a brief journey from west to east, over the bridge and beyond, a drive I take nearly every week, weather permitting. Once you have cleared the toll booths on the western shore, the sounds of your car tires rolling over the bridge joints create a quick staccato on the ascending approach, slowing to a lumbering rhythm at the bridge crest, only to regain an accelerated cadence as you near the opposite shore. Only one lighthouse is visible from the bridge, Sandy Point Shoal Light, built in 1858 and still operational today, faithfully offering a solar-powered white light beacon at six second intervals.

The eastbound span rises nearly 200 feet above the bay at the highest point, curving gently from the western shore to allow for maritime traffic. This unexpected curve was incorporated into the bridge design to enable ocean-going freighters easier navigation between the bridge stanchions. This curve, rising in an arc above the bay's surface, often intimidates less experienced drivers, earning the bridge the undeserved nickname of "scariest bridge in America".

From the bridge spans arching over the shipping lanes, you can view the water below just to the south, dotted with tankers and freighters, sitting, awaiting entry to Baltimore's harbor, their floating parking lot sharply contrasting to the few single-masted white-sailed boats hugging the bay's edges in the distance.

The downward slope of the bridge returns you to land, and in autumn, you are welcomed with a cascade of color, foreshadowing the departure of the agricultural season. The Route 50 corridor winds east and then south and then east again, tree-lined, framed by loblolly and eastern white pine, towering red and black oaks, fast-growing poplars, dazzling maples. As you continue eastward, local produce stands, soon to be abandoned, punctuate the landscape, extending their season from tomatoes, sweet corn, and peaches to pumpkins and chrysanthemums, local jams and jellies. Over weekends, these local outposts become busy stopovers for stocking-up by day-trippers returning to the cities and suburbs.

And interspersed between these family-run stands, old-growth forests, sanctuary for growing herds of white-tailed deer, skirt the plowed, now fallow, fields. The deer only venture from the safety of the sheltering oaks and pines at break of day or dusk. If you scan the fields' edges, where the forest meets the plow, you can find them, often by the tens and twenties, in sharp juxtaposition to the behemoth yellow or red tractors decorating these very same fields, sitting silent, sentries awaiting the final field clearing before the hard freeze of winter.

For it is the early morning hours over my years of travelling across the bridge and onto the Eastern Shore that I treasure. Whether it is sun sparks bursting through the fog-shrouded bridge towers or the showering of white light over the glistening marsh flats bordering the Nanticoke River or even the flare of the sun's inexorable climb above the Atlantic horizon, the spectacle of a new day never fails to engage my imagination. Vibrant and authoritative, painting hues of orange, red, yellow, pink and gold in ever-evolving patterns across the eastern sky, the sun soon bursts into blazing brilliance overshadowing the receding colors. You must look quickly for they are gone in an instant.

More bridges are in your eastbound future, each an additional step away from the stress and intensity of the cities of the Western Shore: Kent Narrows, high and arched, allowing passage of boats without need for a drawbridge, providing easy access to waterfront restaurants renowned for their seafood and sunsets. The Choptank River Bridge, entry to Cambridge, brown information signs enticing you to history and nature, to historic Christ Church or the Blackwater National Wildlife Refuge, home to resident nesting bald eagles and migrating flocks. The Nanticoke River Bridge, long and curving, skirting Vienna, its height providing views of expansive river marshes sliding into the bay. If you glance skyward, you often score the sight of a lone bald eagle, in desultory swooping and soaring, circling high above the river's waters.

And as you drive further east toward the rivers and bays that flow into the Atlantic, take time to stop waterside to inspect the edges of a marsh or the curve in a hidden bay, for it is at this magic brightening hour that the shorebirds engage. An osprey, often mistakenly called a "sea eagle", climbs and plunges, talons ready, seeking a glint of fish but disappointed in its search. A cormorant dives, repeatedly, only to eventually surface with a wriggling eel that is bent on escaping an early morning fate. The eel wins out. And just as dawn breaks, the tiny armada of buffleheads, often numbering six to eight pairs, glides into the protected waters of the coastal bays and rivers. The antics of these small black and white ducks, diving into shallow waters searching for crustaceans and mollusks, only to pop up twenty seconds later, yards away from where they had entered the water, provides welcome quiet amusement.

Early autumn is the time to travel east across the Bay

Bridge, for as the winter draws near, throughout November and into December, the sunrises more often emerge subdued with slate grays, pale blues, more drab than silver, bringing forth field-hugging fog, delivering only the unbroken promise of eventual light.

You may have already seen the signs, "Chesapeake Country Scenic Byway", their yellow black-eyed Susan's enticing you to take an unplanned turn. And perhaps you have even, accidentally, navigated along portions of the carefully laid-out route. Once you have crossed the Chesapeake, you realize why locals refer to their slice of Maryland as "God's country". Accidental travel on backroads has taken me through towns I never knew with names that hold the prospect of undiscovered stories…... Reliance, Harmony, Eldorado.

I grew up in Baltimore, able to pick a mean crab by age ten and shuck an oyster by age eleven. I have travelled through 48 of the 50 states. While I love my mid-Atlantic state for its diverse geography, for its proximity to the culture of major city centers, and for its geographical position in a weather-protected "sweet spot", often free from the earthquakes, wild fires, tornadoes, hurricanes, and paralyzing blizzards that bedevil other states, I am most grateful for the natural wonders seemingly suspended in time, once I cross the Chesapeake Bay Bridge.

I was born in Maryland, Cumberland actually, when I had no choice of geography. Today, having lived in Connecticut, Texas, and Virginia, and having journeyed to five continents, I choose Maryland.

You're Probably a Southern Marylander If ...

By Liz Cooper

Forty-five years ago, my husband Dave and I moved from New York to St. Mary's County, Maryland. In his quest to become a 'Southern Marylander,' Dave convinced me to embrace the local culture. His argument centered around the fact that we wouldn't want to be considered outsiders. After all, our future children would be born here.

"No problem," I assured him, "I ride the NYC subway every day. I know how to blend in."

He looked at me thoughtfully. "Living here won't be like living in New York, but maybe you'll fit in eventually."

I found this statement slightly insulting, but he was right. Over the years, I became a Southern Marylander. It's hard to explain what that means, but here are some of the lessons I learned.

#1 You're probably Southern Marylander if your dinner is staring at you.

Every state boasts regional specialties. I had heard that Maryland was famous for Chesapeake Bay blue crabs, but I had never even seen one, much less tasted one. When we were invited to our first crab feast, Dave was thrilled. Learning how to pick the crab meat out of the shell was the first step in becoming a real Southern Marylander.

We arrived at our host's back yard, and sat down at one of the long tables covered with brown paper. There were cute little wooden hammers and rolls of paper towels on each table.

"The crabs are running!" Somebody yelled.

I instinctively lifted my feet off the ground to avoid being run over by the herd of crabs I envisioned stampeding past. Luckily nobody noticed as a large basket full of red steaming crabs was dumped out in front of me.

"How come these are red?" I asked. "I thought they were supposed to be blue."

Everybody within earshot laughed. Apparently, they thought this perfectly logical statement was funny.

"They're cooked," my husband whispered. "Act like you know what you're doing."

"Dig in!" our host said enthusiastically as he grabbed a crab from the pile and started expertly whacking away with his hammer.

My enthusiastic husband followed suit, smashing his crab too hard, resulting in bits of shell and crab meat flying everywhere, most of it landing on me. As I picked the pieces out of my hair, I had the creepy feeling I was being watched. As it turned out, a particularly large crab in the pile appeared to be staring at me. He looked a little like my Uncle Fred.

"Sorry, Fred," I whispered, as I daintily picked Fred up by the claw and dropped him in front of me. I froze with the mallet raised. I just couldn't eat the poor little guy. After all, we were family. Our host came to the rescue with the assurance that he had an alternative crab dish I was sure to love. I hoped it didn't involve hitting anything with a hammer.

"Linda," he yelled, "Bring out a softshell sandwich

for this city slicker."

They proudly presented me with something I can only describe as shocking. It was a whole crab caught after just shedding its shell. This softshell crab was deep fried and proudly presented on a hamburger bun. All the claws and feet (feet?) were sticking out. It reminded me of a mummified tarantula. Suddenly, Fred was looking pretty delicious.

"Hey Dave, give me that mallet!"

I smashed Fred to pieces and enjoyed every bite.

#2 You're probably a Southern Marylander if you buy a bag of chicken necks.

When both sets or our parents were coming to visit our new home in Ridge, I suggested we make reservations at a local restaurant. Maybe one that served crab cakes which I had recently discovered didn't require tools to eat.

"Heck no! I'm going to cook them a great dinner. Look what I got," he said triumphantly. He brandished a plastic bag filled with chicken necks. I was stunned.

"I'm not cooking that and to be perfectly clear, I'm not even going to stick around while you do," I stated vehemently. "Who on earth eats chicken necks?"

"Crabs do. These little babies are bait for catching our dinner. There's nothing like fresh crabs from the Chesapeake Bay. All you do is tie a string to them, dip them in the water and Voila! Instant Crab feast. Now that we are Southern Marylanders, we need to serve local specialties. It'll be great. You'll love it!"

I was skeptical. "How on earth do you get that thing on a hook? We don't have a fishing pole."

"You dip it into the water from a string. The crabs will come to you," he said jubilantly as he attempted to tie a string around the first neck he pulled out of the bag.

It must have been slippery because it popped out his hand, shot across the room, and landed in the dog's dish. Felix was thrilled. Dave chased him around the house for 30 minutes trying to retrieve his precious crab bait.

Later, after a long hot afternoon on a dock on the Potomac river, we still hadn't caught anything. I had fun though, watching the commercial crabbers pulling up crab pots chock full of crabs. "The crabs are running I said with authority."

Dave scowled. "I must have gotten the wrong kind of chicken necks."

"Yeah, I countered, there are so many different kinds to choose from."

#3 You're probably a Southern Marylander if you feel the urge to stuff a ham.

After the unsuccessful crab expedition, Dave decided we should serve stuffed ham instead, which is a St. Mary's County specialty. We bought our first corned ham from the local grocery store that very same afternoon. If you've never heard of corned ham, it's because they are only available in St. Mary's County and are used specifically for stuffing.

Originally, it is thought that slaves came up with the concept to make the poorer cuts of ham they were given more palatable. Many families in St. Mary's County have recipes for this dish that have been handed down for generations. There was no internet at this time, so I had to beg my neighbor for her secret recipe. After she thought about it, she told me that anything we New Yorkers cooked wouldn't remotely resemble or taste like her stuffed ham, so there was no harm in giving me the recipe.

Stuffing the ham sounded simple enough, but it is incredibly time-consuming. First, you chop up kale, cabbage, onions, and a lot of spices, including hot pepper. Then you stab as many X's into the ham as you can without splitting the ham apart. Next, the vegetable-spice concoction is stuffed into the X's. The whole shebang is finally wrapped in cheesecloth and boiled for several hours. The cooled ham and stuffing are usually served in a sandwich. What my neighbor forgot to tell me, is that your hands will burn and smell like hot pepper for at least three days. Rubber gloves are a must.

When our parents arrived, they were rendered speechless by the sight of the pile of chicken necks and small mountains of leftover chopped veggies all over the counter and floor, not to mention the pile of dirty dishes in the sink. The large cloth-covered ham sat cooling on the counter. Not to be too graphic, but It was reminiscent of a mummy's head. Our parents promptly insisted on taking us to a restaurant.

They don't know what they missed. After cooling the ham in the fridge and slicing it, it was delicious. It took us an entire month to eat the whole thing. Although we enjoyed it, we never made one ourselves again. To this day, we order ready-made stuffed ham from the local small grocer whenever we get the hankering. Much neater.

#4 You're probably a Southern Marylander if you become an expert on the local historical landmarks.

What better way to be part of the community than volunteering to be a tour guide at the Piney Point Lighthouse? After studying the history of this historic landmark one of a few of the original Donahoo lighthouses left standing, I waited all day in the hot July sun for the dozens of tourists I envisioned lining up for my riveting talk and tour. After two hours, I finally had my first customers. A father and young eight-year-old son arrived and asked to climb up the steep ladder into the top chamber which was an official part of the tour. Unfortunately, it is required that the tour guides accompany any guests who climb the lighthouse ladder. There's a rather large a gap between the top of the ladder and the upper floor. The climb is higher than it looks. As it turns out, I am afraid of heights, a fact I didn't consider when I volunteered for this gig.

I led the way up the ladder, but after reaching the top and climbing into the chamber, I was too scared to come back down. The little boy had to coax me out and back onto the ladder. That was the end of my career as Piney Point Lighthouse Tour Guide. I considered working in the gift shop instead, but I was afraid I would keep buying all of the lighthouse bric-a-brac. Years later, I'm still using my lighthouse potholders, wall hangings, Christmas ornaments, nightlights, tote bag, and other stuff I bought on my first (and last) as a volunteer.

#5 You're probably a Southern Marylander if you find oysters in unexpected places.

Oysters are an integral part of Southern Maryland culture and an important part of the economy. I haven't quite gotten over an incident that occurred when my oldest son was around four years old. We lived in Ridge at the time and our house was only twenty feet from a deep creek. I kept smelling a foul fishy odor in his room. I finally found what I thought was the culprit, a large starfish we had bought in Ocean City during our vacation. I banished it to the porch outside. Problem solved!

Unfortunately, over the next few days, the smell worsened. I finally traced the odor to a small desk drawer in my son' room. It was filled to the brim with once-live oysters he had collected from the creek. He seemed to think they would make good pets. They were extremely dead. To this day, I can't figure out how he managed this without me knowing. We lived too close to the water to ever let him go outside alone.

#6 You're probably a Southern Marylander if you act innocent even when you're 'knot'.

After saving money in a special fund for many years, we proudly bought a 34-foot motor boat. We named it Bite Me. Being the good boating citizens we were, and not wanting to look like landlubbers, we took a safe boating course. Dave and I both passed the course with flying colors.

Our first boating adventure was to eat dinner at a Virginia restaurant on the opposite shore of the Potomac at the Cole's Point Marina. This maiden voyage lasted about ten minutes. When we arrived at the marina dock, I told Dave to quit giving me orders about how to tie the boat up to the dock.

"I took the same course you did" I said, tying my knot with a flourish. "There. All set. Let's eat."

We walked up the hill and were given a lovely table with a nice view of the marina.

"Oh look!" I said, "There's a boat that looks just like ours."

Unfortunately, it not only looked like our boat, it was our boat. Bite Me was no longer tied to anything and was floating merrily past the the moored boats, heading for the main channel.

 I didn't know Dave could run that fast. Everyone in the restaurant stopped whatever they were doing and watched as he flew down the hill, ran to the end of the dock, and catapulted himself across seven feet of water and into the boat. It was very impressive. When he returned to the table, he seemed a little annoyed at me.

"My knot was perfect," I explained, "You must have

bought the wrong kind of rope."

"Yeah," Dave smirked, "There's so many different kinds to choose from."

#7 You're probably a Southern Marylander if your kayak runs amuck.

After the boating incident, it became clear that I would never be the best 'first mate', so I resigned myself to enjoying the creek side of our property. I acquired a sporty red kayak and tooled around on my own. I was, however, concerned about too much sun exposure. I came up with a brilliant idea. Or so I thought.

Taping a big golf umbrella to my kayak wasn't the dumbest thing I've ever done, but it's right up there. About a quarter mile out, the wind picked up and blew the umbrella inside out and jammed it into an upward position. It acted just like a sail and made paddling more difficult while blowing me off course. I was twirling and forming figure eights all over the creek. This wasn't all bad, however. It gave some of my neighbors something interesting to watch from their decks as I blew by. A couple on a nearby motorboat seemed impressed as I executed a particularly graceful twirl. I think I heard applause.

I missed a set of oyster floats by inches, which was good, but I scared my favorite nesting osprey family, which was bad. A blue heron practically had a heart attack when I got too close to his nest and flew close to my head squawking bloody murder. (If you've never heard them, you can't imagine how loud they are.) Later, one of my sons suggested I get one of those big hats that look like you have an umbrella on your head. You can buy at theme parks. I would, but it might look stupid and I don't like to draw attention to myself. Maybe I'll buy a tube of sunscreen.

8 You're probably a Southern Marylander if you say, "De-by-Gawd-Capin."

Some of the local St. Mary's Countians have their own special dialect. It took a while for me to understand what was being said but once I did, I loved it. The pronunciation of some words are unique. Many of the phrases are rather charming. The best example is "Indeed by God, Captain." In order for this phrase to sound authentic, you need to say it really fast and run all the words together. It means "Yes!" It is a hearty and heartfelt affirmation of whatever is being talked about.

Even after forty-five years in Maryland, I don't know if Dave and I qualify as real "locals" or "natives." After all, compared to many families who have lived here for generations, we are newcomers. It doesn't really matter though, because St. Mary's County in Southern Maryland has been a wonderful place to live and we plan to call it 'home' for many more years to come. Therefore, I am a Southern Marylander. De by Gawd Capin!

LIZ COOPER lives in St. Mary's County on the Potomac River. A retired school system reading supervisor, Liz enjoys writing humorous fiction for children. She recently finished her newest book, *Bluebell Skinks Wheelchair Kid.* Website: www.lizcooperauthor.com

Memoirs

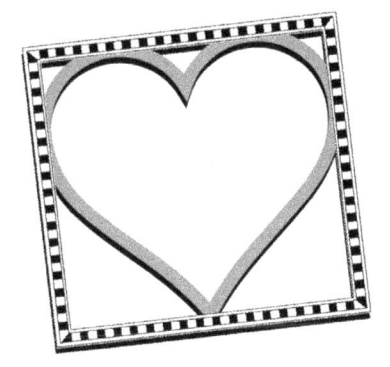

Chasing a Murderer

By James Burd Brewster

In June of 2002, our oldest son stood in the center of the wagon wheel ruts made by prairie schooners as they came up out of the water after crossing the Platte River and declared, "I know real people walked here 150 years ago." Up till that point we had visited a number of historical places where things were "similar to" or "very nearly like" how it was "back then." For Ben, standing in a place where he knew, for certain, his progenitors had walked was very meaningful.

I am like my son in that regard and one of the things I love about Maryland is our Southern Maryland connection with the life and death of Abraham Lincoln. Every night when I commute home from work, I am very conscious that I am traveling on the same roads that John Wilkes Boothe traveled on as he plotted, carried out, and then fled from the murder of President Abraham Lincoln.

Following in Boothe's footsteps is a day-long family excursion. It starts at Ford's theater in Washington, DC, where Lincoln went to see Our American Cousin. You watch the video, tour the exhibits, and then step out into the theater opulent in white trim, white walls, and red velvet seats. Your eye is drawn to the gold drapes over the President's box and you gape in wonder at the place where the President's murder occurred.

"Right there in that seat," you tell yourself and

imagine yourself sitting in the seat you are standing next to and what you would have thought when the shot rang out. Then you remember Ford's theater was used to store personnel files during World War II and the weight of the files collapsed the floors and everything fell into the basement. The entire theater is a recreation and not an exact recreation at that, so that it was not "right there in that seat," but only very "similar to" or "very nearly like" how it was "back then."

The shot rings out. Boothe leaps from the box to the stage. He delivers the last line of his acting career, "Sic Semper Tyrannis." Having broken his leg in the jump, he hobbles out of the theater to the street where a horse is being held for him and flees towards the Navy Yard Bridge. Quashing your urge to pursue Boothe, you help tend to the mortally wounded Lincoln and assist in carrying him across the street to the Petersen House, which remains intact. You place him crosswise on the bed he will eventually die in and watch a doctor attend to him. Then you remember, the real bed is in Detroit and this bed is only "similar to" or "very nearly like" how it was "back then."

Someone reports that Boothe got through the Union Army checkpoint at the Navy Yard Bridge, has crossed the Anacostia River, and is heading down his escape route into Southern Maryland. You speculate he will attempt to evade capture by crossing the Potomac River. Realizing you cannot help Lincoln, you hop in your car and swear you will catch the murdering actor before he escapes into Confederate Virginia. You race down MD 301 to Surrattsville; its name change to Clinton, MD is decades away. Surratt's Tavern is on Brandywine Road and Mary Surratt is a Confederate sympathizer. Boothe has stayed in her tavern. If anyone knows Boothe's plans, she does. You burst through the front door, glance around, and move into the Tavern. Mary is antagonistic but looks guilty as hell. You find the secret compartment where guns and food had been hidden for Boothe. Then it hits you. Boothe was here, in this room, plotting the murder of the President. But, Boothe and David Herold, an accomplish, are not here. They are fleeing south, fast.

You run out of the house on the gravel path; that's where Boothe and Herold ran. You drive down Surratt's Road; that's where Boothe and Herold rode their horses. The route takes you to Brandywine and then to Dr. Mudd's house. Waldorf was farmer's fields then, but Bryantown is a vibrant community center. You suspect Boothe, with a broken leg, may have gone to Dr. Mudd for help. Only Poplar Hill goes left off Pinefield Road and only one road goes right past Dr. Mudd's house. If you are right, Boothe, with throbbing leg, and Herold on weary horses took these two roads to Mudd's house and you are on them now.

Mudd's white two-story home with green trim, surrounded by garden and fields, is off to the right. The stable is gone, but the driveway is the same. You are on your guard as you enter the house, because you don't know if Boothe is here or still one step ahead of you. He is not in Mudd's surgery. You climb the stairs to the second floor using the banister for help. In one bedroom there is a bed you can tell has been slept in, but Boothe is not here. Cursing your luck, you stop at the top of the stairs and realize you have just trod the steps, grasped the railing, and gazed at the same bed that John Wilkes Boothe trod, grasped, and slept in. You demand to know which way Boothe went and notice a servant surreptitiously pointing down a dirt path.

No fool you, you take the hint and pursue the path to the road to Samuel Cox's house. You can't get in his house, but it still stands and so stands your knowledge that Boothe and Herold were on Bel Alton - Newtown Road trying to find a place to hide. Sam hid them in a nearby pine thicket and gave them food. You feel their nearness as you continue your hunt on Faulkner Road and then Popes Creek's Road. You stop at the Postmaster's house, now part of the Loyola Retreat, and ask to see the postmaster, another Confederate sympathizer. He's not in but you find out he stashed a rowboat in Nanjemoy Creek for Boothe and Herold to use in crossing the Potomac. Hoping the boat is still there and that you can catch the two, you run to the gully that leads down to the creek and stand where the boat was tied to the shore. It's gone, but once again you know with certainty that Boothe and Herold stood right where you are.

 Lacking your own boat, the only way to pursue the two into Union-held Northern Virginia is to cross the Potomac River using the bridge at Swan Point and intercept their trail. Good fortune is with you. The entire country side has been alerted and any stranger sticks out like a sore thumb. Boothe and Herold have been spotted at the Garrett farm near Bowling Green. By the time you get there Herold has surrendered, Boothe has been shot, and the shed they were hiding in burned to the ground. At this point, the trail ends and you have come full circle back to where things are "similar to" or "very nearly like" how it was "back then."

 That's when I remember there is one more trail I can follow where, "I know real people walked here 150 years ago." As I retrace the route to my home in Southern Maryland, I am following the path Federal troops took while escorting Herold and Surratt to Fort McNair in Washington for detention, trial, and eventual hanging along the wall that borders 2nd Street.

JAMES BURD BREWSTER learned to walk in Albany, NY, to sail on Lake Champlain, and to navigate a Polar Icebreaker in the U.S. Coast Guard. He is the successful author of the Uncle Rocky, Fireman picture books (www.Gladtodoit.net), the happy husband of Katie Spivey from Wilmington, NC, and the proud father of five grown children. Jim and Katie live in Southern Maryland which is a stone's throw from Washington, DC

Shallow Roots
By Theresa Wood

I'm not from here.

I'm not from anywhere. It's the curse of being a military brat, not really having a home. All my life I thought that home was where my family was, but the truth is much more complicated. For a long time, I thought my home would be my father's hometown. But family drama eventually ruled that out. A hometown, I finally reasoned, didn't have to be the place you were born, nor did it have to be a place you inherited. Although I didn't know where home was, I was determined to find out, no matter how long it took.

My family moved to Maryland in 1981 after spending the previous few years living outside of Athens, Greece, and at first I resented having to move to Maryland at all. It had taken a while, but I had come to see Athens as my home--as much as any military kid can call anyplace home--and leaving it at the end of eighth grade was difficult. By the time school started a few months later, my friends from Greece had stopped writing letters and I set about creating a new chapter in my life. Although I often had friends, I also spent a lot of time alone and struggled to fit in.

My parents decided to retire here. Maryland had everything they wanted in a home: four seasons, history, access to cultural and sporting events, and a varied landscape. I wasn't convinced. At twenty-two, and wrapping up my college studies, I was considering where in the world I wanted to live, debating whether I wanted to stay in one place long enough at all for it ever to be called "home."

Then I met my soon-to-be husband at a college party in the early months of 1989. We began talking as if we had always known each other, but had not seen each other in years and so were merely catching up. One of the things that attracted me to David--in addition his unabashed appreciation for John Denver's music--was that he lived on a farm a couple of hours south of campus. I had grown up romanticizing the family farm, often dreaming about living on one. Sitting in the backseat of our family sedan with my two brothers as we drove through rural America on many trips to my dad's hometown in Wisconsin, I longed to live on a farm. I imagined generations of extended family members living close to the land, working shoulder to shoulder for the success of the farm. Perhaps that idea was so seductive to me because my own family seemed like a collection of random parts, each of us locked in our own rooms, our own worlds; or, if we were together, we watched television in silence, save for whatever conversation could be crammed in during two-minute long commercial breaks. I began to think, talking to David that night, that it was my destiny to be part of his extended family and to raise our children on that farm, working side-by-side for eternity. His home would become my home. I abandoned all plans to leave Maryland, and from then on I rarely passed up the opportunity to drive down from the Baltimore suburbs to St. Mary's County on the weekends to join him.

Back then, the farm was still primarily in the business of growing tobacco. That wasn't so unusual, as tobacco had been the single-most profitable crop in

Maryland since its founding in 1634, sometimes being used as currency itself. Most farms continued to grow tobacco centuries later. It is a labor-intensive process, starting with the sowing of seeds in several large beds in January, and covering them with cotton and plastic; setting the young plants in the field in the spring; watering them and tending to them until, in a good year, the plants grew to be over six feet tall; topping them by slicing off the flower to encourage more leaves to grow; cutting and spearing the stalks in the summer months; and, finally, hanging them to dry or cure in the barn until the winter. One crop overlapped the other. Winter months were spent in the packing shed separating the leaves from the stalks and tying them together in bundles, then laying the bundles one on top of the other until the pile was fully sandwiched between two woven wooden pallets, or pads. It was a fragrant, if dusty job. These pallets were loaded onto trucks and taken a few miles up the road to Hughesville where buyers came to set the price and purchase this particular strain of tobacco, Southern Maryland Type 32, which was created to thrive in the sandy-clay mixture of soil found here. Most of the tobacco sold here found its way to overseas markets. While that crop was on its way, a new one was already in the ground.

During the spring of 1989, I frequently sat with Dave, his mother and siblings on a six-seated planter where we were sometimes joined by his grandmother. I loved the process of planting tobacco--picking up handfuls of seedlings from the metal basket in front of me and separating the finger-thin two-leafed plants from the knot of dirt-clotted roots to place them one at a time into the grabber that rotated upwards and opened up to receive them. As Dave's father Joe pulled the planter behind his John Deere tractor, the plants were placed in the ground at regular intervals and given a drink of water from the hose attached to the planter's basket.

His grandmother Millie often shared stories of her life growing up on her own family farm, and her time as a young newlywed on this one, while we worked. The rhythmic clacking sound of the forked pincers where we placed the plants provided background music as we heard about her efforts to help her husband plant tobacco back during the Depression, following behind as he pegged the field by poking the ground with a metal-tipped tobacco stick. Her job was to take a seedling from the bag she carried and drop one in each hole before covering it up with dirt. It certainly seemed like he had the easier of the two jobs, and I was grateful for the machinery that allowed the job to be so much easier now than it had been. Over the course of many hours and many days, we left behind us a string of green jewels, a testament to our teamwork.

Being on the planter was everything I dreamed it would be. Even though I hated smoking, I rationalized participating in the work of the farm because this was their family business. David's great-grandfather Harry had purchased this farm back in 1920 or so and raised their nine children on it. When they passed, the farm was parceled out to each of their nine adult children and David's parents worked very hard to buy the shares from them so as to restore the farm. They worked the land over many decades and continue to work today, although the crops have changed since the state offered tobacco farmers a buyout in 2000.

I loved the feeling of dirt caked under my nails at the end of a planting session, as much as I relished each of the family stories that were related to me during the course of our work. This was the first time in my life I had done any kind of work with my hands, the first time since I was a child that I had intimate contact with dirt. I felt as though I were being initiated into the family. I had a purpose. I belonged here.

When planting season ended, there was a pause in the work as the plants were nurtured into maturity. Much to my disillusionment, though, the rest of the work on the farm—topping the plants, cutting and spearing them, and hanging them to cure in the barns—was left to the men. The women went out shopping or did housework. This traditional division of labor was unacceptable to me, a modern college-educated woman, and I was determined to show all of them that women could hang with the men, if they would only try. After all, Millie had shared a lot of stories about helping her husband through the entire season. What had changed, I wondered, as I began to think of ways to prove that it could be done. I wanted to prove that I was no weak or pampered girl, but a strong woman, just like his grandmother had been when she was my age.

One morning in July, I woke to find myself alone in the house. It took a moment to realize that David's mother and sister had gone out to the store and the men had gone out to the fields. At first, I was disappointed at not being included in the shopping expedition, but then I saw this as my opportunity to prove my worth. I quickly got dressed and pulled my hair back before walking across the road to join David.

I stood at the edge of a field of tall, green tobacco, struggling to find him amid the foliage. The broad leaves of the tobacco plants swayed in breezes so subtle they didn't make a dent in the beads of sweat gathering on my forehead. Each plant was graced with a pastel pink flower, with trumpet-shaped blooms heralding their presence. They reminded me of the fire red-orange blossom of the wild trumpet vine draped along the shoulder of the road and snaking up the electric poles, only more stately and elegant. Millie had laughed more than once when looking at these trumpet vines, beautifying the world for free when they cost so much in her gardening catalogs.

I found Dave between two rows of plants, shirtless and wearing red cotton shorts with a green John Deere ball cap and brown leather work boots. (We would definitely have to work on color coordination!) He was bent over, striking at something near the base of each plant with a hand ax, before taking a step toward me and repeating the process. When he reached the end of the row he stood up and asked, "What are you doing here?"

"I came to help," I said and smiled.

"You know, girls don't usually help with this part." He wiped his forehead with the back of his axless hand.

"I know, but I'd like to try."

He smirked and said, "Okay," motioning for me to follow him to his truck. He rummaged around the back before finding another small ax. I took it from him and we walked back to the field. He showed me how to identify the suckers at the bottom of each plant and how to strike at them without harming the stalk. Doing so keeps the main stalk and leaves from having to compete for sunlight and water. He cautioned me against damaging the leaves, the money part of the plant. Then, he walked to the next row over. We agreed to meet at the other end.

In his row, he was also taking off the flowers, or "topping" the plants. In any other context, they would be called beautiful, but here they would be sacrificed. As pretty as they are, they inhibit the growth of the plant. Inwardly lamenting my lack of a green thumb, I sighed, but I couldn't tell what was a sucker and what was part of the plant itself. I considered calling over to Dave for help but decided against it. I didn't want him to think I was dumb or helpless. I took my best guess and swung. The plant was still standing and a small hanger-on fell off. I shrugged, pausing only to wipe at the stream of perspiration threatening to blind me.

After whacking at a dozen or so plants, my hand started to hurt. I thought it was just a muscle cramp and kept on with my work until the pain grew too intense to continue. I stood up and tried to open my hand. It was closed so tightly around the wooden handle that opening it was a struggle. I gasped as the air hit my palm and dropped the ax.

"Dave!"

"What is it?" he asked through the wall of tobacco separating us.

"My hand," I uttered. It had begun shaking. I stared at the oozing wounds on the pads of my palms. All of them had blistered and torn.

Dave walked over and inspected my injuries. "It's okay," he said. "Happens until your hand gets used to it."

Gets used to it, I thought. I hadn't considered the fact that this work would lead to calloused hands. "I think I should go back to the house."

"No, it's really easy to take care of," he said, squatting down and grabbing a handful of dirt which he rubbed into the angry red sores. I winced, shocked at this treatment, which he assured me was a typical remedy. When he was done, he picked up my ax and handed it to me.

I stared in disbelief. "I can't," I said. "It hurts too much."

He shifted the tool to my left hand and grinned. "You're left-handed, aren't you?"

I stared at him a minute longer, not sure if he was testing me or if I was simply failing my own test. I took the ax with my left hand and he returned to his row. I turned around and continued to work on the suckers, this time stepping backwards as I made progress. It wasn't long before the familiar numbness, followed by burning pain, set in. I stood up and opened my throbbing left hand, which was now shaking and oozing as well.

"That's it," I said. "I'm going back." I walked to the end of the row and Dave met me there. He saw my left hand.

"You can't go back until we take care of that," he said.

"You are not rubbing dirt in this one."

"No, but you have to wash up. Each of the plants here has a resin, which will stain your skin. Come on." He started walking to the house and I followed, fighting back tears from my painful failure.

We stood at a deep sink in his parent's garage. I held up my useless hands while he turned on the hot water and picked up a bottle of bleach.

"Are you crazy?" I asked, pulling back my hands.

"It's necessary," he said, taking my left hand and pouring bleach over the raw wounds, rubbing it in and rinsing it off. I stifled a scream, not willing to appear any weaker than I already had. He repeated the process with my right hand, then turned off the water and picked up a dirty pink towel from a nearby hook. He wrapped my hands in the towel and patted them gently.

"Not so bad for your first time," he said, smiling at me. I managed a weak smile, but said to myself that this was also my last time.

I went back inside the house while Dave returned to the field. I packed up my things and debated whether or not to stay for the rest of the weekend as planned.

Then the women returned. They laughed at my shredded hands and I did too, embarrassed at my own arrogance and ignorance. His mother Mary apologized for not waking me up--she wanted to let me sleep, a statement which caused her daughter (who had been awakened hours earlier than she had wanted) to roll her eyes in silent complaint.

That afternoon I helped unpack groceries and together we got dinner started, something I was not allowed to do at home as the kitchen was my mother's domain. The warmth and coziness of the wood-paneled kitchen in the middle section of their split-level home was hypnotic. I had a newfound appreciation for women's work, and for the first time since being in my grandmother's home in the late 1970s, I felt as though I were home. Maybe there was a place for me here after all, even if it wasn't going to be alongside my man during topping season.

David and I married in 1990 and moved down to the farm. In the early days of our marriage, we both worked full-time office jobs, and he worked nearly full-time on the farm. I spent a lot of time alone and staring across the road at the long dirt road and lush green fields that had lured me here only to have abandoned me. For a while, I started thinking back to that February before I met Dave and wondered where else I might have gone in this world if I hadn't been distracted by romance.

Elsewhere in the county, my outsider-status was apparent as soon as I opened my mouth. "You're not from here, are you?" lifetime residents would ask, suspicious because I carried a county surname like a wolf in sheep's clothing. I would never fit in here, I thought.

But I refused to give up. Once I had children, I thought, St. Mary's County would feel like home. Their home would become my home.

Within a few years, the county itself began to change as the expanding naval base brought tens of thousands of newcomers, chain restaurant parks, and strip malls. My children's home bore little resemblance in many ways to the county their father had grown up in. Even the farm itself has changed since taking the state's tobacco buyout and now grows grapes, corn, hay, straw, vegetables, and apples instead of tobacco. A large row of greenhouses hides a nursery of annuals that each year are sent for resale to a network of home-improvement stores. A shop on the farm sells local produce and honey, and in the fall there is a corn maze and hayrides. My in-laws remind me that we have to constantly create, and be open to reinventing ourselves if we are to survive. They recently celebrated the farm's century mark and are still going strong.

My children are nearly grown and the nest is approaching empty. One has already decided to live elsewhere in the state, and another may move to Tennessee. My youngest plans to stay in county on some days; but then there are colleges in other states that she likes too.

Millie, their beloved great-grandmother, passed away a few years ago. She was the first family member to accept me, literally with open arms when we first met. Her home was always open and she was always willing to share stories of her life, her past, herself with anyone who was willing to listen and to accept her as well.

In many ways, after nearly thirty years, I remain an outsider, the only one living on the farm who is not originally from here. No one says anything about it, but I'm always aware of it.

Yet, Maryland is home. It has taken traveling to Europe, and across the country more than once, getting away and seeing this place from a different perspective, talking about it with strangers, for me to become comfortable saying that. Each time I went somewhere new, I also kept my eyes and heart open for a sign that some other place was my true home. I thought I would know it as soon as I arrived, crossing the city limits or county line and feel a pull in my gut like a magnet. I thought I would hear a song on the breeze and instinctively know

I was home. That, of course, has never happened. Whenever and wherever I travel, I'm relieved to head back to St. Mary's County. There's been no fanfare or epiphany, just the quiet acceptance that somehow I've grown roots here, and while they stretch mighty far to allow me to wander, they always manage to pull me back here.

Every year, when the trumpet vine blooms, I'm reminded of Millie and her amazement that people would buy the trumpet vine from a catalog and plant it on purpose. But, that doesn't surprise me. The trumpet vine, once it's established, is difficult to get rid of. Its roots run deep--but that's not the only reason plant is successful. The roots also grow away from the vine, anchoring it in place and allowing it to roam. Wherever the vine itself touches the ground, it grows a new set of roots. These roots don't necessarily burrow into the ground. They can draw in moisture and nutrients from the air.

Hardy and tolerant and low-maintenance--perhaps that's why this plant has no particular home. It flourishes nearly everywhere in the eastern United States, across six or seven agricultural zones. And, while it has some drawbacks (it can become aggressive and unwanted in some places), it has certainly adapted well to the loamy soil of St. Mary's County. So have I. This is my home.

THERESA WOOD lives in St. Mary's County with her husband, three children, two dogs, and a cat. She is a middle school English/Language Arts teacher, who grew up loving books and writing. She has lived in Maryland for over thirty years, and still enjoys exploring new and familiar places in the state.

Lawbreakers

By Aly Parsons

We had waited until midnight before venturing into the park. My husband had a blanket over his shoulder. I grasped his arm above his bent elbow with one hand and held my white cane in the other, depending wholly on his night sight as we pussyfooted off the asphalt onto the grass. He relaxed his arm, signaling me to step halfway behind him as we walked a zigzag course.

Giggles burst out around me and several voices said, "Shhh."

I held in my own giggles. I was in my late 30's, yet I felt like a child who had snuck out of the house after curfew.

Marveling at this unplanned gathering in the middle of Silver Spring, Maryland's largest unincorporated city, I waited while Paul spread our blanket. I found two edges and sat where I'd have room to stretch out beside him. We removed our jackets and balled them up as pillows--the August night was warmer than predicted.

A child's voice said, "Ooh!"

The dark held the swell and ebb of murmurs, the occasional sweet sound of liquid filling a cup, and the wafting aroma of hot cocoa.

I whispered, "Can you tell how many people are here?"

Paul sat up and I could feel him shifting around. Then he lay back and said into my ear, "Over 200."

And they stayed so hushed!

My low vision was worst at night, but I could just make out the leafy tops of trees fringing the park, slightly lighter than the sky's blackness. The park was in the middle of a residential area. No lights shone from any of the houses. Perhaps all the residents were out here with us.

Several small parking lots abutted the park, and I occasionally saw the flash of headlights that went out a few seconds before the sound of wheels rolling on gravel stopped. Car doors opened and shut, oh, so quietly.

We all knew the park was closed after sunset, yet new arrivals kept swishing through the grass from all directions. I guessed which parking lots the police might pull into. If they came and the crowd rushed for the other exits, Paul and I would be among the last to get out, sure to be caught.

We hadn't been able to resist coming out for the show. I lay on my back staring at the sky, ever hopeful. As fulltime workers, we were lucky that the peak of the Perseid meteor shower was occurring on a cloud-free, moonless Friday night. The Perseids could be seen in the northern hemisphere each summer as earth's path intersected comet dust that flared through our atmosphere as exceptionally swift shooting stars. But this year it was extraordinary. Every hour, over 400 meteors were supposed to be visible. Indrawn breaths around me attested to when clusters of falling stars were most brilliant.

I searched and waited, smiling when a short streak crossed my narrow field of vision. With partial sight in one eye and total blindness in the other, I couldn't follow its race across the sky, which was fine. Back when I had normal sight, I'd never viewed the Perseids.

People had probably crept into every park that had open space to watch this spectacle. What I most loved about Maryland was the abundance and variety of the parks that were available (even when we weren't supposed to be there).

Eventually, there was more movement around us, people leaving while fewer arrived. Paul nudged me, and we gathered up our blanket. By then the air had chilled and we were wearing our jackets.

When we reached our car, Paul said, "It's too late to go to bed. I could use some coffee."

"For some reason," I said, "I have a craving for hot chocolate. How about an early breakfast at the Tastee Diner?"

During the short ride to our 24-hour landmark diner in Silver Spring, Paul asked, "Were you able to see any of the meteors?"

I said happily, "I saw three!"

At 4 a.m., we arrived at the diner. The restaurant was crammed. Some people had thermoses on their tables, and the rich scents of cocoa and coffee permeated the air. I could see nearby faces well enough to know that the smiles of a shared experience were being flashed from table to table. The sense of community warmed me while I waited for my hot drink.

ALY PARSONS' works are online and in anthologies. A version of "Lawbreakers" is in *Behind Our Eyes 3*. An Odyssey Workshop graduate, she has led a writers' group since 1980.

"We Don't Have a Head of Household:" Collective Living in Baltimore

By Fred Pincus

Although most people in Maryland live in fairly conventional households, I experimented with collective living in the 1970s. I had arrived in Baltimore in 1968, fresh out of graduate school, to teach sociology at University of Maryland Baltimore County. Being single, I lived alone in the Bolton Hill section of Baltimore for several years.

I grew tired of solitary living so began to explore the various forms of group living that had sprung up around the city and country. *Countercultural communes* emphasized living "liberated" lifestyles that included "smashing monogamy," eliminating "bourgeois privacy," using drugs, eating natural foods, etc. People in these communes, sometimes called "hippies," did not necessarily engage in political activism to end militarism, racism and sexism. Their alternative lifestyles were the hippies' political statements of rebellion.

Political collectives, on the other hand, used a different model of political activism. For example, about a dozen people from the University of Wisconsin moved into South Baltimore in 1970 to do community organizing in what was then a white working-class community. They bought three small houses, pooled their incomes, shared household tasks and expenses to provide political support to promote their activism. Of course, sex, drugs and natural foods were sometimes included in some political collectives.

My introduction to the countercultural model of living came in 1970 when a colleague and I attended a conference in Bloomington Indiana. After a long car ride, we arrived at the address that we were given for housing at around 2:00AM and knocked on the door. A young man, wearing only a towel, opened the door to greet us and showed us to our sleeping quarters on the second floor. In the decent sized bedroom, lit by a few candles, 8 twin-size mattresses sprawled on the floor.

"Take your pick," he said.

Sue and I looked at each other and one of us said, "We don't want to take anyone's bed."

"Having your own bed is bourgeois," he replied. "We just take whatever is available."

"Right," I said with some hesitation. "Where is the bathroom?"

"It's over there," he pointed, "but you are not permitted to close the bathroom door. It's one of our few house rules."

"Okayyy," I said, wondering what I had gotten myself in to.

Sue and I selected two adjacent mattresses, went to the bathroom (separately) and tried to fall sleep in this strange situation. I leaned over to Sue and said, "I have a confession. I closed the bathroom door." "So, did I," she replied.

It was difficult to sleep since our host was having noisy sex with a woman in the corner, a few yards away from us. Two large German shepherds kept chasing each other across the mattresses. At one point, a woman crawled into bed with me and quickly excused herself when she found the mattress occupied by a stranger. After this experience, I knew the countercultural model was not for me.

During the summer of 1971, I decided to take the plunge into more politicized collective living when two political comrades and I moved into a two-story, three-bedroom row house in the Northwood section of Baltimore near Morgan State University. Both were women and we were all in our twenties.

Chris and Mary were graduate students at Johns Hopkins University. We all belonged to the Baltimore chapter of the New University Conference (NUC), a national radical organization that had around 1000 members around the country. Although living with two women may sound like countercultural heaven, it was all pretty innocent. We each had our own bedroom and were each romantically involved with people outside of the house. Both women were independent feminists, so we rotated cooking, cleaning, laundry and other household chores. Chris and I did political work together and we occasionally got high together. In contemporary terms, we were housemates and friends "without benefits."

I remember trying to explain my unconventional household to my very conventional Aunt Blanche on one of my visits home to Los Angeles. Blanche was a hairdresser and always trimmed my hair when I visited. As I sat in a chair in her bathroom, a towel over my shoulders, she asked,

"So, what's it like living with two women?"

"We're just friends. It's no different than living with two men."

"Do they cook and iron for you?"

"No," I laughed, "we take turns. They're feminists."

"Oh," she said with a puzzled look on her face. "Don't they get jealous of one another?"

"There's nothing to get jealous about."

"Doesn't your girlfriend get jealous?"

"Oh, no. She comes to visit and stays over."

After a few moments of silence, Blanche shook her head and said: "I guess it's a new day."

Our collective living also caused minor problems for the federal government. As we were sitting in our living room one afternoon, a well-dressed woman in her 50s knocked on the door. She introduced herself and said she was from the Bureau of Labor Statistics of the U.S. Department of Labor. Our house had been randomly selected in the national survey that determines unemployment rates among other things.

Chris and I were thrilled since we used these statistics in our teaching and research. Mary went along for the ride. One of the first questions was a standard question: "Who is the head of the household?" The poor woman had no idea that she had just entered a minefield.

"We don't have a household head," said Chris, firmly. "We are a collective and all of us are equal."

"I have to indicate one of you as the head of household," she replied. "There's no box to check for 'collective.'"

"No one is the head of our household," said Mary.

"Whose name is on the lease?" she asked, hoping that this would solve the problem.

"All three of us signed the lease," I replied, smiling.

"Who earns the highest income."

"Fred does," said Chris, "but that doesn't make him head of the household. We share all decision making."

"Look," the interviewer said dejectedly, "one of you needs to be head of the household for the purposes of the survey."

"How about if Chris and Mary flipped a coin?" I said.

"Okay. Ok." she said, shaking her head.

Chris became our household head for the day. The rest of the survey proceeded without incident. The woman returned a month later for a follow-up interview. Before she began, I said:

"We want Mary to be the head of household this time."

The interviewer gave me a stern look and said: "You can't change the head of household from one month to the next."

"Why not," I said. "Chris won the coin flip last time so it's only fair that Mary be household head this time."

"Please," she said, "can we just get this done." Since she had her job to do, we agreed.

Chris and I enjoyed sharing the house, but Mary was less involved, so we looked for new people to live with. In the summer of 1973, Chris and I moved into a 3-story, 5-bedroom row house in the Charles Village section of Baltimore with Howard, Carol and their teenage daughter, Linda, to begin a second political collective. I had met Howard and Carol at an NUC meeting in the Midwest shortly before they moved to Baltimore from Iowa because Carol got a job teaching at UMBC.

Two main political activities were based in the house – The Great Atlantic Radio Conspiracy, a half-hour pre-recorded radio program that aired on WBJC-FM; and Research Group One, a small publisher of pamphlets and research reports. Although we never officially named our collective, we were an anti-capitalist political group that included feminists (Chris and Carol), an anarchist (Howard) and a Marxist (me). Linda, fifteen years old, was more countercultural.

We shared the rent and expenses as well as the cooking and household chores. The adults were not countercultural in that we had separate bedrooms and respected each other's privacy. Howard and Carol were a couple, I was dating a woman from New York City, and Chris had several relationships outside of the house.

Brightly-colored political posters lit up the walls in the common areas of the house– "End the War," "Fight Imperialism," "Women Hold Up Half the Sky," "Racism Divides the Working Class." Howard's collection of political protest buttons, pinned to bulletin boards that hung on the walls, greeted people as they entered our home. Our bedrooms reflected our individual politics and personalities.

We all liked good food, so our culinary standards were very high. Part of a friendly competition, each of us put a lot of effort into our cooking – only once every four days! After a long day of teaching and meetings, I would come home and know that a wonderful meal awaited me. Howard was a connoisseur of low-cost wine that always complimented our meals.

We also rotated other tasks such as dishwashing, shopping, laundry and cleaning. No one liked doing dishes after I cooked because I used a lot of pots and pans. Since we were all pretty responsible, I grew to appreciate the benefits of sharing household tasks.

We had a lengthy discussion of how to handle paying for rent and household expenses. "From each according to ability, to each according to need" was an ideal, as was pooling our incomes. Ultimately, we contributed to household expenses based, in part, on our ability to pay. Since my modest salary was the highest, I paid the most.

There was always a lot to talk about since we were all involved in overlapping projects. We debated articles in *The Guardian* and *In These Times* as well as other political periodicals. We went to demonstrations together and offered advice about our individual and collective projects and studies. Howard, Chris and I were sociologists, so we discussed various professional issues.

Carol regularly taught a course called "Sex Roles and Inequality," one of the early women's studies courses in the country. We decided to team-teach, so I introduced a course called "The Sociology of Women." We taught together twice in the early 1970s and learned a great deal from each other. We respectfully debated the differences between feminist and Marxist analyses of gender issues in front of our students and we provided good role models about how a man and woman can act together as equals. Living in the same house facilitated the planning process and provided lots of dinnertime conversation.

One night, we were talking about a radical student name Sharon.

"She's doing a really interesting project for an independent study," I said.

"What's that," said Carol.

"She's developing a feminist board game."

"What!" exclaimed Carol.

"The idea is to move around the board and earn liberation points," I replied. "She's done a lot of research into feminist history."

"She's doing the same project for me in another class," shouted Carol.

"Yikes. She never told me that. She's ripping us off."

The only real negative about the collective is that we made the worst real estate decision of our lives. When we moved in, we could have purchased the house for a mere $10,000. After some discussion, we decided to rent since none of us were sure how long we would be in Baltimore. A year later, we offered to buy the house, but the owner no longer wanted to sell. Some 20 years later, Howard (who was the only one still living there) finally bought the house for more than five times the original amount.

During these early years in the collective, I felt integrated and whole. We were living and working cooperatively for common goals and we liked, respected and supported each other. There was always someone to talk to, but I could retreat to my bedroom when I wanted to be alone. When my girlfriend came to visit, everything I cared about (outside my family of origin) was in that Baltimore house. I was happy.

In 1972, I had begun to date Natalie, a sociologist who taught in New York City, and I spent many weekends in the Big Apple. I was a part-time member of the Baltimore collective. In the summer of 1974, Natalie and I got an apartment together and I began a one-year sabbatical leave in New York. After the sabbatical, I began weekly commuting to Baltimore and lived in the collective until 1980 when Natalie came to Baltimore for her one-year sabbatical. We sublet a furnished house a few blocks away from the collective and spent a pleasant year there. When Natalie returned to NYC, I stayed in the house during the week and shared it with two Johns Hopkins University students. It was a financial arrangement, not a political one.

My Baltimore living situation at the end of January 1981 changed again when I moved in with Ann and Fred, our next-door neighbors in Baltimore. Natalie and I had gotten friendly with them during her sabbatical in Baltimore and they had an extra room. Fred was an engineer and Ann was a school social worker who had gotten her degree at UMBC although her main job in 1981 was taking care of their two pre-school daughters. This was not a third collective living situation since I was simply renting a room in their house, although I did help with shopping and cooking from time to time.

Ann and Fred were liberal, church-going Christians, something dramatically different than my Jewish atheism. We knew this about each other and felt that this wouldn't be a contentious issue. We did, however, have to work out one issue: They began each meal by saying a prayer while holding hands at the kitchen table, something I didn't feel comfortable doing. We talked about it before I moved in.

"What about if you bowed your head and held hands with us but didn't say anything," Ann said.

"That works for me," I replied, "but what do we tell the kids when they asked why I wasn't saying the prayer?"

"That's a good question," said Fred.

"We could tell them that I didn't believe in God," I suggested.

"No," Ann said firmly. "I don't want to do that. What about if we say that you are Jewish?"

"I'm ok with that," I said, "but some Jews pray before eating and I have some Jewish atheist friends who hold hands silently for a few seconds before dinner."

"I think our girls will be satisfied with just saying you are Jewish," Ann replied. "Let's not make things more complicated than they have to be."

And so, it was. The girls would have to wait to learn about atheism. It was great to develop a relationship with two young kids since Natalie and I were still having issues about having children ourselves.

Our son was born in September 1982 at the start of my second one-year sabbatical in New York. One year later, when I got in my car to return to Baltimore for the fall semester, tears came to my eyes. This would be the first time I was away from Josh for several days and I would miss him terribly.

My living situation in Baltimore had changed once again. This time, I would share an apartment with three other radicals at the Progressive Action Center (PAC). A group of academic and professional radicals, including Natalie and I, had purchased a vacant 3-story library building in Waverly from the city in 1981 for $1000 and put $50,000 into renovations, financed, in part, by a low-interest city loan. The PAC opened its doors during my sabbatical.

The main floor looked like a small library and housed the Alternative Press Center, an organization that indexed radical periodicals. Several offices of other movement organizations and a print shop were also housed on the main floor. The Red Wagon Day Care Center occupied the basement.

At the back of the library, a door led to the living room and kitchen of the apartment. The four bedrooms and bathroom were on the second floor. The four occupants each paid the same rent.

As I unpacked, I had an epiphany: *"I'm free from childcare responsibilities! I only have to deal with myself!"* Although I felt a little guilty that Natalie was still stuck with Josh back in New York, I was also extremely happy. I had the best of both worlds: a father and husband for half of the week and an unattached person for the other half. What could be better than that?

The culture of the PAC apartment, which had developed over the previous year when I was in New York, differed from my previous collective living experiences. First, there was an open-door policy which meant that people from the PAC constantly wandered in and out of the apartment. I hated it and convinced my housemates to adopt a closed-door policy where those who did not live in the apartment would have to knock on our door before entering.

Second, there was no set meal schedule and people were spontaneous about eating. This was a drag because I had to cook more often. I suggested a schedule of cooking/eating but no one was interested.

The semester began, and I settled into my new digs until a bombshell struck. Cliff and Kim, two of my housemates, announced that they were pregnant and planned to raise their child in the apartment.

First, I was stunned. So much for my best of all possible worlds. Then I was pissed. There was no way that I was going to live with someone else's baby when I have my own to go home to! My carefully planned living situation was disintegrating.

I called a house meeting and addressed Cliff and Kim: "This isn't an appropriate place to raise a child. It's not safe; there's no handrails on the stairs; it would be hard to babyproof." I went on and on.

"I can put up rails on the stairs and do whatever else needs to get done to make the place safe," replied Cliff. Kim agreed.

Then I turned to my two other roommates. "It's going to get noisy here. There's going to be lots of baby stuff all over the place." I continued enumerating some of the hassle that goes along with babies, but to no avail. Although neither had lived with a baby before, they were interested in trying.

I lost on all counts. As I retreated to my room to lick my wounds, I knew I had to find another place to live. I didn't want to move back with Ann and Fred, even if they would have me. Been there; done that.

I called Howard and he was delighted with my moving back. My old room, it turns out, was still available and the rent was low. I moved the following week.

Howard had gotten divorced and his daughter had

moved to San Francisco. Chris had completed her PhD and taken a job at the University of Washington. So Howard and I were housemates and often shared meals during the two or three nights that I was in Baltimore.

I lived with Howard for another 13 years until Natalie and Josh moved down to Baltimore, permanently. We bought a house in Mount Washington and lived as a conventional nuclear family. I enjoyed collective living when I was younger, but it was time to move on.

FRED L. PINCUS is an Emeritus Professor of Sociology at the University of Maryland Baltimore County. He has been a political activist for many years and is presently trying to find a publisher for his memoir manuscript. He lives with his wife, Natalie Sokoloff, in the Charles Village section of Baltimore.

MARYLAND, MY MARYLAND

By Margaret Warfield

The southeast corner of Baltimore County where I grew up was dominated in the early and mid-1900's by Sparrow's Point's Bethlehem Steel Mill. When my Norwegian grandfather immigrated to America, he got a job at Bethlehem Steel. He had been a rigger on a sailing ship and helped raise the first smokestacks on the new mill. This was at the turn of the century. Coincidently, Anton Halvorsen's great grandson, my brother's son, worked for the company that razed the mills in the 1990's.

Most of my relatives and neighbors worked at the mills. My mother, grandmother, and aunts often sat around our kitchen table, visiting and gossiping and drinking tea. What I remember about the conversations was the men in the families were always referred to by where they worked in the mills. "You know Charlie Kelly at the Wire Mill, or Mr. Stanton in the Shipyard, or old man Luffy in the open hearth, or that poor Tom Bloom in the sheet mill, or Ratsy Wright on the railroad." These men worked shift work. Neighborhood kids knew not to play near a house where the father was sleeping during the day; he had worked all night. Life was predictable when you worked at the Mill. Kitchen calendars marked the hours of each shift, marked the hours of the steel workers' life.

We also mark time by the change of seasons. I knew

it was fall when my Welsh grandmother, Annie Williams Halvorsen and her sister, Mae Cunningham, put on their best black dresses, hats and gloves and took my cousin Anne and me to lunch at Hutzler's tea room in downtown Baltimore. I remember that my grandmother's hat was black straw with a small veil and bunch of cherries on the brim. I thought she was wonderful. It was my favorite day of the year. We rode the #26 streetcar from our house to downtown. I loved the ride though the neighborhoods: Greek, Russian, Polish, Irish, Italian, German. Row houses. Painted screens and white marble steps. Churches on every corner. After lunch the sisters took us to the shoe store on Lexington St. to buy black patent leather Mary Janes for church and sensible brown leather shoes for school and we had our feet x-rayed!

Winter meant sledding and ice skating and building a snowman in the front yard. Spring was the Flower Mart at Mount Vernon Place with the ladies in their wide brimmed straw hats selling bouquets of flowers and The Baltimore tradition of lemons with peppermint sticks for straws.

School was out in June and the anticipation of our annual summer vacation with my Cunningham family to Ocean City was more than I could bear. Magical Ocean City. Riding the waves on blue canvas rafts, body surfing and jumping the waves. Sitting on the beach every day under striped umbrellas and surrounded by the unmistakable fragrance of Coppertone lotion. Our mothers slathered us with suntan lotion; we still got burned.

Ocean City food was the best: candy cotton and Dolle's salt water taffy, Dumser's ice cream, limeade and hot dogs at Beach Plaze where the cute college boys worked. And then dinner at Phillips Crab House, a tradition. We always got steamed blue crabs, corn on the cob and butter for dipping the chunks of backfin crabmeat.

From an early age a Maryland child is taught the CORRECT way to open and eat a hard crab.

In the evening we would walk the Boardwalk. Just walk and watch everyone else walking and watching us. Summertime in Maryland—life didn't get any better.

I was Maryland born, raised, and educated from first grade to a BA from McDaniel College in Westminster. I taught school in Baltimore County and Baltimore City. I married my college sweetheart in Maryland. My family and his family lived in Maryland. We thought we would never leave Maryland. But in June of 1969, 8 hours after we were married in the chapel of Goucher College, we were in our 1967 Mustang Convertible heading West. We left family and friends and all that was familiar and beloved to us: black-eyed Susans, "Save the Chesapeake" license plates, brick homes with front porches, our widowed parents, the mid-Atlantic's mild 4 season weather and the most beautiful state flag in the union. Our destination was Los Angeles CA where Bob had recently been transferred.

Westward Ho! With great anticipation we motored over the worn Appalachian Mountains, travelled hour after unending hour through corn fields and mid-west plains, crossed the ragged Rockies, plunged into Death Valley's desert and finally to California.

In Baltimore I had lived in the Bolten Hill neighborhood in the center of the city. I was urban-wise—or so I thought.

L.A. overwhelmed me. The city and surroundings were one moving phenomenon where cars traveled 90 mph down 6-8 lane freeways all day, every day. Nothing ever stopped. Constant motion.

And forget the myth of a perfect climate. It is an arid desert. No beautiful rolling green hills like Carroll County's. no sailing on the Chesapeake Bay, no grandma's lovely English flower garden. I learned about zero gardening-rocks, sand, and cactus. There were extremes—no rain for months which meant dry brown brush in the hills. Then the mountain winds came, igniting the brush into wildfires. In January there was torrential rain for days and days. The result: mudslides on the denuded hills. Then, it started all over.

But for a brief period of time each year, the winds would change direction and blow the smog (smoke and fog) out to the Pacific and the days were glorious. It didn't last long.

The cycle would begin again.

And besides the deadly smog, and adverse weather, the earth shakes in California. IT LITERALLY MOVES! I COULD FEEL IT!

We awoke one morning, and the bed was rocking as if we were on a rolling sea. There was silence in the house except for the dishes rattling in the cupboards and the pictures banging against the walls. The epicenter was 90 miles from our house. Aftershocks continued for weeks We FELT them, too.

Bob and I began to make plans. We quit our jobs, sold our house, rented a big U-Haul truck, and loaded our possessions. Our neighbors came over to "meet" us. We had been in the neighborhood for a year and had only met a handful of people living on our street. One of them was from Maryland and had gone to school with my brother. One neighbor said, "I've seen a lot of people come to California. You are the first we have seen leave California. Good-bye, we said. Good-bye walled yards, good-bye stucco houses, good-bye earthquakes, and crowds and cars and cactus, good-bye smog.

Off we went through the Arizona desert, over the Rocky Mountains, through the Plains and cornfields and

Kansas farmlands, over the Appalachians and the soft green hills of Virginia, across the Chesapeake Bay, along the marshlands of the Eastern Shore and finally to Ocean City. We arrived on the Fourth of July 1971, two years after we left. We Celebrated. We were home. We sang:

"From hill to hill, from creek to creek
Potomac calls to Chesapeake"
MARYLAND, MY MARYLAND"

MARGARET WARFIELD: Although I was raised and educated in the Baltimore area, I have lived for the past 48 years in Ocean City. Two children, and three grandchildren are my greatest pride.

The Tribes of Port Baltimore
By Walter Curran

March 1976

Working on the waterfront means learning to deal with tribalism, in all of its forms. Each port has its own unique flair, its own tribes and its own dialect. In Baltimore, the largest tribes are Irish, Polish and African-American, sometimes called Micks, Polacks and Blacks. The tone of voice of the speaker determines whether it is a descriptive adjective, harmless banter or vitriolic acid, thrown at the recipient. It's amazing what you can tell from the tone of someone's voice.

When dealing with the waterfront, there is a hierarchy, a union, the International Longshoremen's Association. The big Kahuna of tribes. There are also local unions, tribes within the tribe. What helps define them as tribes is everyone is related to most of the others in that tribe, whether through blood, marriage or long-standing family feuds.

Growing up near the docks in South Boston, I already knew about the Micks. No secrets there. I am one. Now, in Baltimore I have to learn the ways of Polacks and Blacks, cultures I know about, but only from a distance. On the waterfront there is bias. Large chasms difficult if not impossible to cross, but to limit it to skin color ignores the true nature of the rift. On the Baltimore waterfront, the personal bias has little to do with skin color but everything to do with culture.

I admit, first day on the job, there is trepidation on my part. Four years of being at sea with crew members of many cultural heritages have given me a glimpse at how important "commonality" is in our everyday lives. Find something in common with the folks you work with and focus on that. By focusing on the common ground, other things, potentially disagreeable and even explosive, get set aside and tolerated. They still exist, but are no longer 'triggerable' by an inadvertent word or misinterpreted look. On the waterfront, the common ground is hard work.

As the new guy on the block, bearing a strong, New England accent, I am an outsider. Tribalism exists within the management ranks also, with the Irish being leery of the Polish. Blacks don't exist in management. They hold positions of leadership in the unions but haven't broken the tribal barriers of management.

My tribal barrier to entry is language. I don't speak "Balmorese." For example, the third time the secretary in the office called me "Hon," I felt obliged to explain to her I am a happily married and wouldn't succumb to her charms. By the twentieth time, I understood that they called everyone "Hon," your given name was incidental, and I no longer felt the need to fend off amorous advances that existed only in my mind. Big sigh of relief, followed by, "Hey, why doesn't she think I'm the cat's meow?"

The Port of Baltimore comprises different geographical tribal areas. Downtown, predominantly Blacks, is the inner harbor, beginning to convert to tourism as the old piers either collapse or get torn down. Locust Point, both North and South, are predominantly Irish. Both North and South terminals are break-bulk terminals that can also handle containers. Western Maryland piers abutting South Locust Point are old and purely break-bulk.

Dundalk, a large Polish area, is king. The Maryland Port Administration (MPA) has put most of its money into the building of Dundalk Marine Terminal to handle the newer container and Roll-On / Roll-Off ships. Different parts of the city, different neighborhoods, different cultures, different tribes.

I had arrived at the Dundalk office on Friday afternoon and checked in with my boss. Booked into the Days Inn in Towson where I would live for three months until my wife and kids could join me, I spent the weekend driving around town, familiarizing myself with the city. I've been here before. The first time on my training cruise in 1964. The "Block" the ultimate den of iniquity, was the highlight of that stop. I had also stopped here a few times when I sailed as a Third Mate. When here as a deck officer on a freighter, your perspective is different. You're leery of the longshoremen, presuming they will damage the cargo or the ship or try to steal things. Now, after working as a stevedore in Boston supervising those same longshoremen, I knew they were just guys, earning a living. No different here in Baltimore.

Cargo doesn't appear by magic. To load cargo on a ship, it first has to arrive at the pier carried by trucks or railcars. Vice versa for the cargo discharged from ships. Handling that cargo is hard, demanding work. Depending on the type cargo, it might have to be hand-thrown, like bags of coffee or cocoa beans weighing over one hundred pounds, or handled with a forklift if palletized or crated. Someone also has to count that cargo and verify it's correct. Here is where the 'tribes within the tribes' comes into play. The counters are the clerks and checkers.

The clerks/checkers union is Irish with a smattering of Polish. They are responsible for all the clerical work required for the proper receiving and delivering of the cargo, both to and from the ships, trucks and railcars.

Clerks work in an office, checkers work outdoors on the pier and on the ships. There is a rigid seniority system for getting a job, but on the job, it's the Chief Clerk who controls your fate. All tribes have chiefs, but the Chief Clerk is more of a Shaman, able to work magic. For example, putting his brother-in-law who has a tough time tying his own shoes on a tallying (counting) job. When said brother-in-law lets the tally slips blow away into the harbor while lighting a cigarette and sneaking a nip out of his flask, magic is required to make the counts come out right.

That same Shaman also has the magical ability to interpret time. When a checker he doesn't like or one who screwed up the counts too many times in the past shows up two minutes late on the job, there is a reaction. The Shaman sitting at his desk, without lifting his head, will point at the clock on the wall and say, "Try again tomorrow, I've called for a replacement." The miscreant slinks away, knowing it is futile to argue. When the Shaman's poker partner shows up forty minutes late, the only statement made is "Did you bring me a donut?" Tribalism!

The car-handlers union is Black. They don't handle cars. That is a throwback reference to railcar work. The car-handlers do all the physical work of loading and unloading trucks and railcars. Everyone in the car-handlers union is old. Very old! Ancient! Some of them can barely move. The foreman on our pier, exaggerates egregiously, telling blatant lies about his prowess in everything from sex to sporting events. He is one of those who can barely move, except for his jaw, which never stops. He is a legend in his own mind.

More importantly, he is respected by the other car handlers and the checkers. If there is a problem with a car-handler, it is instantly resolved when the foreman shows up. It may take him half an hour to get there but the resolution is instantaneous. He is slow but effective. Knowing what a difficult work environment the waterfront can be, and knowing no one gets respect on the waterfront without earning it, I will respect him.

The longshoremen's union, called 'the big local' is Black, Irish and Polish. Back in the day, a "Stevedore" was an individual with knowledge and experience at loading and unloading cargo and the Stevedore would hire and direct longshoremen. Now it is a generic term for the companies who hire longshoremen. Every stevedore company has a certain number of 'gangs' assigned to it, called 'house gangs' and the company has first call on their services. Every gang has a foreman (Gang Boss). If not being used by their 'house' company, gangs may be assigned to other, competing, stevedore companies. This is the best example of management ignoring tribalism. Every gang carries its reputation, good, bad or indifferent. Management wants the gang that works hardest, often preferring another company's gang over one of their own. Another form of tribalism.

To complicate matters further, each individual longshoreman can work for any company on the waterfront and will get his job on a daily basis through the hiring hall, based on his seniority.

Prior to my arriving at Baltimore, the longshore union was split into two locals, one black, one white. A legal proceeding resolved that and they formed one local, but there still exists Black Gangs, Irish Gangs and Polish Gangs. There is some mixing when an individual doesn't show up for work and they order a fill-in replacement from the hiring hall, but, by and large, the tribes stand apart.

The Gang Boss, like the Chief Clerk is a law unto himself. If you screwed up on the job and embarrassed the Gang Boss, you'd sit on the sidelines for a month or more before he'd hire you again. Although the seniority system is cast in stone, the Gang Bosses are hammers that break the stone when it suits them. If you complain, you are ostracized, sometimes silently, sometimes vociferously. Few complain. They know the price to pay.

Notice I keep saying "him", 'his,' or "he." Here in Baltimore, in fact, on the entire east coast there are no women in the waterfront tribes. There are rumors of a few brave souls trying to break into the work force. It won't be easy. Machoism is alive and thriving in all tribes on the waterfront.

Monday morning, clear weather, fifty-two degrees. Considered cold in Baltimore, this is a warm day in New England. Same temperature and humidity, different attitude.

No ships working this morning, only terminal operations. How do I handle the tribalism? More important, how will they handle me? My boss introduced me to the chief clerk, car-handler foreman and cooper foreman. A cooper is a carpenter, known as a wood-butcher. A lot of minor repairs are necessary for the cargo. Broken crates, slits in bags to be sewn up. This morning, we are also stripping containers. No, not some illicit or immoral activity. Stripping is unloading the cargo that arrives in containers. A driver backs a container into one of the truck platforms at the transit shed. The checker checks the seal to see if it is intact and records the number of the seal. The longshoremen open the container door, same as a truck door, and then unload it. Two tribes working in unison. The car handlers don't touch the cargo until after it has reached a place-of-rest on the transit shed floor. It's called "jurisdiction" and is the biggest source of arguments on the waterfront. The tribes are not always friendly to one another.

Today, first day, two-and-a-half hours on the job, I lend a hand to a longshoreman struggling to open a sticky container door. Normally, they don't allow management to do anything that is "union" work for fear you are trying to replace them, but no one minds when you give them a hand with something. He had unlatched the door handles, one on each of the two rear doors, but couldn't get the door to move. I reached in and grabbed the edge of the door along with him and we heaved. It moved an inch and froze. I prepared to give another heave when the longshoreman who I later became good friends with, slammed the handle in frustration, slamming the door on my left hand catching the middle finger. OUCH!

I pulled the hand back and gingerly peeled off my work glove. Half an inch of the finger was crushed.

"Geez, Cap." Everyone one in a position of authority is labeled Captain. "I'm sorry."

Grimacing, I responded, "It's okay, shit happens. Just keep going here." I went to the chief clerk's office, told him what happened and went to the company office. They filled out a few forms, and I drove myself to the hospital. After the usual emergency room frustration, the doctor decided they needed to snip a piece of bone off to get a clean closure to the wound. I said "Fine, let's get it over with." Two hours later, I drove back to the pier, the middle finger half an inch shorter than before. I finished the day, hurting, but I'd rather be busy than idle.

That night, in the motel room, the finger throbbed. The doctor had said to keep it elevated. Easy to do when awake but sleeping is another thing. I thought ahead and borrowed two #10 nails and hammer from the cooper at the pier and took them to the motel room. At bedtime, I took my belt and looped it, then hammered in one nail at a steep angle through the belt hole just above the headboard on the bed. I wrapped a facecloth around my left wrist, slipped it into the belt loop and tightened it. Voila, an elevated hand all night long. Wary of the maid seeing it, I didn't know if her tribe would be friendly, I removed the nail every morning and reinserted it into the same hole at night.

For the next two weeks, whenever anyone asked me how I was, I gave them the finger, making sure I smiled when I did so. That I came back to work the same day, never complained and made a point of telling the longshoreman responsible for the gaffe it was my fault for not paying attention, helped me get accepted into the waterfront. I didn't plan it that way, but it worked. The icing on the cake was when I told them about my belt-in-the-wall story. A couple guys agreed that maids can't be trusted. I didn't ask how they came to that conclusion. Now, even though a member of management, I am one of the guys. Today, I get my feather and am unofficially inducted into the Baltimore segment of the "Micks" tribe.

OCTOBER 2018

Forty-two years later, I now follow the tribes on Facebook. Not much has changed.

WALTER F. CURRAN is a retired maritime executive living in Ocean View, DE. He has sailed on merchant ships and worked on and around the docks in Boston, Philadelphia, Baltimore, Jacksonville and San Juan, P. R. A member of the Rehoboth Beach Writer's Guild, Maryland Writer's Association,, and Eastern Shore Writer's Association, Walt has self-published two novels, *Young Mariner* and *On to Africa* as well as a book of poetry, *Slices of Life-Cerebral Spasms of the Soul.* He is currently working on his third novel of the *Young Mariner* trilogy.

Christmas Eve Celebration
By Joanne Zaslow

We walk in the front door singing "hello" to sofa-sitting teens. They look up from iPhones and The Hunger Games to smile and shout back "hello!" echoed by dogs barking from cozy spots under arms or legs. Inhaling the clove and sugary scent (ham? cookies?), my husband, Hal, and I stroll into the kitchen to join other family members. A shouted "Woohoo!" floats up from the basement as our kids and their cousins—all over age 20, some married with children—slam glasses on the bar after they've hoisted peppermint shots. In years past, I've witnessed their mutual affection during this practice, which goes back many years, but not as far back as Lea and Steven's annual Christmas Eve Celebration.

—

"Let's pile the gifts in the car. I'll get the pasta salad from the fridge; you grab the sodas, OK, Babe? Mere, would you sit cross-legged on the car seat? Some gifts need to go on the floor. Joel! Come down, Joel! Time to go to Aunt Lea and Uncle Steven's for Christmas Eve!" So begins our annual trek to Eldersburg, MD, to Hal's brother's home.

When we arrive, our niece, Kara, welcomes us with: "You're late!" and helps carry our packages through the front door. We all wave hello with elbows and blow kisses to Hal's folks, Al and Ruthie, who, rubbing dogs' scalps, look up from the soft leather sofa and grin.

On route to the kitchen, we glimpse Bud's walnut cake, Barbara's cheesecake and her gym bag overflowing with dog treats, Mahjong, and a communal surprise for all family members—one year it was a red sweatshirt imprinted with the family tree representing everyone, including the dogs.

Setting the pasta salad on the kitchen table, I kiss cheeks of family members already enjoying Sophie's crab dip and Steven's HOT picante sauce made from Lea's homegrown tomatoes. Gifts in hand, we clamber down to the basement, where more kids are hanging out—rolling Hess trucks, playing video games, and stuffing down hands-full of Lea's chocolate chip cookies. Hal's sister, Mindi, and her husband, Ron, snap countless photos as our kids join theirs or snuggle into the plush sectional sofa to read by the fireplace. Soon, Mindi, with help from our nephew Marc will rally all cousins to decorate the fresh Christmas tree.

Dinner's an endless feast, as is talk about dem Os, school, work, trends—through board games, hot coffee, and neighbors dropping by. At midnight, everyone gathers in the basement around the pool table to open gifts. After the kids, the adults take turns presenting, opening, ogling, and weeping over our Secret Santa's gift to us—such as Steven's gift to his dad of the evergreen bush pinned with sorely needed cash, Mindi's framed photo for Barbara declaring her love for her sister, Marc's eight-man tent to Boy Scout leader Hal.

At 2:00 a.m., we're still hugging and laughing as we repack our cars, including the cookies and deli sandwiches we grabbed for the road.

A Christmas Eve celebration is not unique, except at this one, almost everyone is Jewish. Initiated decades before by my in-laws to welcome their Catholic daughter-in-law, Lea, into the family, the celebration has thrived—through decades and contracting and expanding family. Our grandchild, due any moment now, will be blessed to take part in the comfort, love, and welcome of this Christmas Eve Celebration.

JOANNE ZASLOW is a seasoned communications professional who, among her other corporate positions, served as long-time director of Editorial and Design Services, American Psychological Association. Zaslow's currently an editorial freelancer who also writes creative nonfiction and co-leads the MWA Teen Writers Club at the Odenton Regional Library.

Greek Easter Bash
By Joanne Zaslow

The day after American Easter, we can buy chocolate eggs and bunnies, jelly beans, and baskets for half price or less, and my family will do it because the crowd will soon be descending on our home in Crofton, MD, for the Greek Easter Bash!

My mom, dad, sister, brother, husband, and I (and later, more family members) will spend weeks preparing. My mom is the general. We check off her tasks, listed in a spiral notebook, as we complete them—from "ask Aunt Jan to bring the ham" to buy paper plates, wash the fingerprints off the walls, hose down the patio tables, rent chairs, hide the Easter candy for the dozen kids under age 12, and make sure everyone—Dad's side of the family, Mom's side of the family, their children, their children's children, everybody's close friends—has been invited.

Our family supplies staples: turkey with Greek stuffing (a ground round, chestnut, and raisin blend); sweet and doughy Greek Easter bread—the recipe handed down to Mom from my Papou (grandfather) who emigrated from Greece in 1913—and dyed eggs aplenty. As the guests arrive, they present their offerings like calling cards: Aunt Margie's pasticcio (noodles layered with ground beef and béchamel sauce), which only she is allowed to cut ("You might break it!"); Aunt Helen's gift-wrapped halva (syrupy squares of baked farina with a cherry in the middle of each square); cousin Dorothy's fixings for the gargantuan Greek salad, which she will prepare in situ in a big production (as her late dad used to) featuring the chopping of spring onions and fresh mint from Yiayia's (grandmother's) garden. The aromas of lamb, yeasty bread, and fresh-cut cucumbers stir my appetite and soul.

As the crowd settles, Uncle Stanly leads the opening toast, thanking my parents, remembering those no longer with us (invariably weeping), and joining in to sing "Christos Anesti" (Christ has risen) before we all hoist, then down our paper cups of Mavrodaphne. We then line up, hugging and hollering over engagement rings, new jobs, and lousy luck, to work our way around tables heavy with the Greek buffet. Dessert and coffee will follow the meal, and we'll indulge in the Greek custom of cracking each other's dyed eggs until a winner—the owner of the egg with the fewest cracks—is declared. As squealing kids play tag and cousin John strums a bouzouki in the living room, family and friends will linger, chatting and joining in endless conversation circles until the last group packs up plates-full of food "for tomorrow" and drives into the night.

The Greek Easter Bash began as a joyous variant to our predominant setting for family gatherings: funerals. Although it metamorphosed with the addition of Filipino, Jewish, and other new family members and delicacies, it thrived in that Crofton home for 30 years. While we miss the old guard, the original families, we honor all, lost and present, by carrying on the tradition, now in my cousin Gale's home, and passing it down to our children.

Baltimore Fairytale
By Karen R. Roberts

Outside Baltimore's 19th century Marburg mansion, while sparkling chandeliers and ornate crown molding furtively peeked through the lace curtains of Number 14, a man dropped a square of linen on the sidewalk.

I met that man in early 2011. He was an elementary school teacher and an army officer in the 450th Civil Affairs Battalion (Airborne), United States Army Reserve. His Match.com profile provided other intel: he liked to travel, he had a horse, he was winding down a six-month course at Ft. Knox. He would be returning to his Baltimore home in a few weeks. We had regular phone dates and corresponded daily.

On our first real date he stated that he would be deploying to Afghanistan in July of 2012. I had shrugged. It was over a year away, let's see where this leads. My telltale heart would've blabbed what I was really starting to feel about this man. I collected photos of us and love notes from him in a folder labeled Paratrooper Ron. I wore a tiny locket with a tiny photo of him next to my heart.

Three months later, on a Montego Bay beach at sunset on Easter, Ron pulled me close and whispered, "I love you."

When you're faced with a deadline and having the time of your life, the clock seems to tick faster.

We packed a lot of living in the next twelve months. We rode horses through the fields of Howard County, ran and biked the NCR trail, competed in a triathlon in Columbia, hiked at Oregon Ridge and Washington Monument State Park. We would alternate hosting breakfast, lunch, and dinners at his Sparks home or at my Homeland residence.

In January 2012, we attended a black-tie event. On the way to our hotel, it finally dawned on me; he's going to propose tonight. Ron had booked an enchanting hotel suite and we would be dressed appropriately for engagement photos. I was practically giddy. I was very careful not to let Ron know that I knew. I would play along, not wanting to spoil the surprise.

As we were getting ready, I poured a shot of wine into a Dixie cup to settle my nerves. I leaned against a chair, putting on my shoes. That's when I spied it. I wasn't wearing my glasses, but on the other side of the counter, nestled in his maroon beret was a substantial glinting object. I quickly clomped to the other side of the room, one shoe on, one shoe off, pretending not to see what he would be sliding onto my left hand later that evening.

A moment later, Ron reached into his beret, grabbed the item, and I watched in astonishment as he fastened the medal onto this uniform. He glanced over at me, whistling in appreciation, as I stood teetering on stilettos, trying to disguise the confused look on my face. He asked if I was ready. Off we went.

On a flight to Aruba, three months later, Ron and I were engrossed in our own thoughts. He was probably thinking of how he would stage the proposal. I was thinking the same. A year earlier, on a Caribbean beach, he had changed the dynamic of our relationship with the Big Whisper. In just a few days, we had another Easter sunset ahead of us. I had confided with my closest friends and my two sisters that Ron would be popping the question.

As soon as Ron and I arrived in our hotel room, he made a beeline to the safe, under the pretext of securing our wallets and passports. I smiled knowing that he was putting my engagement ring in there. I busied myself with unpacking my "say-yes-dress" that I would be wearing in a few days.

Whenever we came back to the room, Ron would go to the safe and assess the inventory. I would gravitate to the balcony or the bedroom, to allow him privacy.

On Easter Sunday, we had a romantic dinner under tiki lights and twinkling stars. Ron asked if I would like to take a walk on the beach. I demurely acquiesced, my heart racing, threatening to divulge my excitement.

The moon beamed down brightly, witnessing our hand-holding that evening. Ron didn't ask me any other questions.

I stretched out in bed that evening, my arms folded behind my head, staring into the darkness. I listened to the waves crash. I came to the realization that Ron was going to wait until he returned from his deployment to propose. Secure in that knowledge, I snuggled up close to him, and drifted into a deep sleep.

A few weeks later, my home phone rang. It was my sister, Nancy. "Hey Karen, I have a seminar on May 4th at the Inner Harbor, would you be available for lunch that day?" Nancy lived in southern Maryland. We didn't see one another frequently, and since my other sister, Linda worked with me, having lunch with both of them was going to be extraordinary.

We made plans. Before we ended the call, she added, "And wear something nice. I know you often dress casual at work. We're going to go somewhere special."

As I was sipping coffee that May morning, I realized my sister was visiting on Flower Mart Day. Flower Mart is Baltimore's oldest public festival, signifying the arrival of spring. It's a boisterous street party where revelers show off Preakness derby hats, chew on lemon-peppermint sticks, and sample locally harvested crab cakes, oysters, and soft-shell crabs.

A portion of Charles Street is closed, local vendors sell flowers, jewelry, art, crafts, and a menagerie of other items; their tables encircling the Washington Monument and along the sidewalks of the Mt Vernon parks. There are contests and entertainment. A little something for everyone.

Early that morning, strolling along Charles Street from my parking lot to my office, I observed vendors setting up for the day. A stage was assembled in the middle of the block, food trucks were lined up on Madison Street. I had been on the Flower Mart committee a few years earlier. I greeted old friends and favorite vendors. It was like the intersection of Mayberry R.F.D. and Cheers; friendly, folksy, everybody knows your name.

I skipped up the steps of 14 West and soon after, I became ensconced in a meeting. I covertly stole glances at my phone, excited to meet up with my sisters. The library clock chimed the quarter hour as I glided out of the meeting and towards my office. Nancy was climbing the steps, intercepting me. Linda was right behind her. Perfect timing.

"Hey, I'm so glad you found my office. I'm sure finding a parking spot wasn't as joyous. I totally forgot what a big day this is. Ohmygosh, it's so good to see you…," I had the speaking pace of an auctioneer.

Nancy gave me a hug; she turned me towards my office. Dominating the doorway was Ron, in his military dress uniform.

I looked from Ron to Nancy, very confused.
"Ron! Aren't you supposed to be in school?" I asked. Ron nodded.

Delicate soprano notes streamed up from the park, "…O'er the land of the free and the home of the brave". Clapping and cheers resounded.

I was discombobulated. My limbic system was having difficulty regulating my varied emotions. Surprise. Curiosity. Delight. Excitement. And a smidgen of anxiety.

"Are you able to join my sisters and I for lunch?" My stomach had already started to grumble, I could smell the barbecue grills that had been fired up hours earlier. I was envisioning talking my sisters into a café table to watch gaily festooned celebrants and their pets parade by, reveling in the pageantry of Baltimore's rite of spring.

"Karen, I have something to ask you."

Ron stepped towards me, swallowing my small hand in his, leading me down the staircase. My sisters parted, letting us pass between them. My eyes were on Ron, assessing his confidence, how good he looked in a uniform. I was proud to be on his arm. My co-workers were admiring Ron as well, their eyes gaping at us over the rails of the staircase, standing in shadowy doorways watching us descend towards the front door.

We reached the first-floor landing. Ron scooped me up in his arms, carrying me down the steps and across the parquet floor. His shoes are very shiny is all that I could think.

A camera flashed. Again. and again.

Slowly, I gained clarity on why Ron was at my office.

Someone ran to hold the door open for Ron, since his arms were full.

Out in the sunlight, the carnival atmosphere abruptly became silent.

Little girls dancing around the maypole froze. Vendors and patrons cut conversations short. All eyes were on the man in uniform, holding the woman in red.

Ron gently set me down on the sidewalk, his strong arms cradling my shoulders, making sure I was steady, before reaching into his pocket for the velvet lined box.

As he knelt down, seconds prior to the world becoming obscured like a kaleidoscope, and tears brimmed in my eyes, I saw the horse-drawn carriage patiently waiting at the curb, a sparkle from the silver ice bucket chilling a bottle of champagne, a bouquet of roses.

Somewhere nearby, on a Bose speaker, a duet by Joe Cocker and Jennifer Warnes played softly.

Afterword

As the carriage clip-clopped down Cathedral Street, the regal couple inside smiled and waved to the well-wishing pedestrians and motorists. Unbeknownst to the woman in the red dress holding a champagne flute, attached to the back of the carriage was a poster containing a photograph of her and her officer and gentleman.

The photo had been taken on a beach, capturing the crimson blush in the western sky. The barefoot couple was engaged in a toast, their champagne flutes lightly touching. In very large print beneath the photo were three magical words: SHE SAID YES.

Karen R Roberts, CPA, PMP, is currently working on her first novel, a collection of short stories, and dabbling in life story writing. When she isn't reading or writing, she's probably singing, sneaking a bite of dark chocolate, or adding copious notes to her idea book. She and her husband reside in Maryland horse country; she is a member of the Story Circle Network, Women's Fiction Writers Association, and the Baltimore Chapter of MWA.

CPSIA information can be obtained
at www.ICGtesting.com
Printed in the USA
FFHW022027270219
50751973-56154FF

9 780982 003268